ST PAUL'S
REVELATION

ST PAUL'S
REVELATION

by: Viola Yassa

ST SHENOUDA PRESS
SYDNEY, AUSTRALIA
2025

St Paul's Revelation

COPYRIGHT © 2025
St Shenouda Press

All rights reserved. Except for brief quotations in critical publications or reviews, no part of this book may be reproduced in any manner without prior written permission from the publisher.

ST SHENOUDA PRESS
8419 Putty Rd,
Putty, NSW, 2330
Australia

www.stshenoudapress.com

ISBN 13: 978-1-7638415-4-3

Foreword

I foreword this book to my Beloved Son Peter and His Family for their kindness and gentle loving care.

May the Lord bless them and shine His Grace upon them always.

PREFACE

Although there is no direct mention of the time when the Jews and Gentiles became separated, it seems that the formal separation of Jews and Gentiles did not occur until God called Abraham to be the father of His chosen nation, Israel (Genesis 12). Many view Abraham as the first Jew, even though the precise term Jew did not come into use until after the return from exile when the tribe of Judah ('Jew'-dah) was dominant. However, since Abraham's son Ishmael was not of the chosen line, and since Abraham's grandson Esau was not of the chosen line, a more accurate placement of the division of Jews from Gentiles would be with Jacob, whose name was changed by God to Israel (Gn32:28). All of the descendants of Jacob, through his twelve sons (the fathers of the twelve tribes of Israel), were members of God's chosen nation. Therefore, it seems most biblically sound to place the division of Jew and Gentile at Jacob, the father of Israel.

In this study, we will look into the mysteries revealed to St Paul regarding God's purpose in history to save His people, both Jews and Gentiles, so that He may be glorified. The study was with St John the Baptist Bible Study Group at the Holy Apostles and St Abanoub's Church, Blacktown, Sydney, Australia.

May the Lord grant us to grow in the knowledge of His Word every day!

Feast of the Cross
September 2016   Viola Yassa

CONTENTS

INTRODUCTION	1
ST PAUL'S REVELATION	7
THE MYSTERY OF CHRIST	27
THE MYSTERY OF THE INCARNATION	35
THE MYSTERY OF THE INDWELLING CHRIST	49
THE MYSTERY OF THE CHURCH	89
THE MYSTERY OF ISRAEL'S TEMPORARY BLINDNESS	121
THE MYSTERY OF THE RESURRECTION OF THE DEAD	143
THE MYSTERY OF INIQUITY	167
THE MYSTERY OF THE BRIDE OF CHRIST	181
RELATIONSHIP BETWEEN CHRIST AND THE CHURCH	191
APPRECIATION OF THE MYSTERY	217
ST PAUL'S CLAIM TO DIRECT REVELATION	227

INTRODUCTION

God first promised the Messiah after Adam and Eve's Fall into sin (Genesis 3). God later confirmed that the Messiah would come from the line of Abraham, Isaac, and Jacob (Gn12:1-3). Jesus Christ is the ultimate reason why God chose Israel to be His special people. God did not need to have a chosen people, but He decided to do it that way. Jesus had to come from some nation of people, and God chose Israel.

God's ultimate purpose for Israel — that of bringing the Messiah into the world — was fulfilled perfectly in the Person of Jesus Christ. However, God's reason for choosing the nation of Israel was not solely for the purpose of producing the Messiah. God's desire for Israel was that they would go and teach others about Him. Israel was to be a nation of priests, prophets, and missionaries to the world. God's intent was for Israel to be a distinct people, a nation who pointed others towards God and His promised provision of a Redeemer, Messiah, and Saviour.

The Jewish people were called, cultivated and conditioned to be a missionary people. Thus, those Jewish people that embraced Messiah would be best equipped to be evangelists and missionaries. The best strategy to catch the most fish is not to do all the fishing yourself, but to recruit the most effective fishermen who can catch the most fish. That central missionary calling of Israel/the Jewish people is that they be a "light to the Gentiles" (Is42:6; 49:6; 51:4; 60:1-3; Acts13:47).

Interestingly, both Jews and Gentiles are mentioned in the account of Jesus' death. The Jewish leaders arrested Jesus, but it was a Roman (i.e., a Gentile) who sentenced Him to death and Romans who carried out the execution. "For He (the Son of Man) will be delivered to the Gentiles and will be mocked and insulted and spit upon," Lk18:32. Later, the apostles prayed, "Indeed Herod and Pontius Pilate met together with the Gentiles and the people of Israel in this city (Jerusalem) to conspire against Your Holy Servant Jesus," Acts4:27.

Gentiles were long seen as enemies of the Jewish people, yet Christ provided good news for both Jews and non-Jews. The prophet Isaiah predicted the Messiah's worldwide ministry, saying He "will bring forth justice to the Gentiles" and would be "a light to the Gentiles" (Is42:1, 6). In Mk7:26, Jesus helps a Gentile woman who had asked for her daughter's freedom from a demon. St Matthew's Gospel begins with a genealogy of Jesus. The genealogy includes the names of several gentile women brought into the people of God: Ruth, Thamar, Rahab, and Bathsheba (the wife of Urias). St Matthew explicitly takes a path through Jesus' ancestry to connect Him with Gentiles and Jews, to highlight the importance of the inclusion of Gentiles in the Kingdom inaugurated by the Messiah's coming.

The Jews became disobedient and stubborn (Rom10:21). They have hardened themselves, consequently, against the two essential features which constituted the Messianic dispensation, a free salvation (Rom10:5-11) and a salvation offered to all by universal preaching (Rom10:12-17). By the sinful unbelief of the nation of Israel (Rom11:12), a shift in salvation history took place from Jews to the Gentiles. It was God's plan to save the Gentiles through the Jewish nation. But Israel failed to function as the light of the world. They made it difficult for the Gentiles to be saved. They despised the Gentiles and called them dogs. The Jews were proud of their privileges and work-righteousness.

Even the newly saved Jewish Christians made the evangelization of the Gentiles difficult, requiring them to bear the heavy yoke of the Law. They demanded that the Gentiles be circumcised and embrace all ceremonial and dietary laws, as we read in Acts 15: "Then some of the believers who belonged to the party of the Pharisees stood up and said, 'The Gentiles must be circumcised and required to obey the Law of Moses'," Acts15:5. St Paul also mentions this in his letter to the Galatians: "Those who want to make a good impression outwardly are trying to compel you to be circumcised. The only reason they do this is to avoid being persecuted for the Cross of Christ. Not even those who are circumcised obey the Law, yet they want you to be circumcised that they may boast about your flesh," Gal 6:12-13.

It was God's plan to save the Gentiles through the Jewish nation. For the most part, Israel failed in this task. The Jews refused to embrace their Saviour Messiah. But God cannot be frustrated. He opened the door to the Gentiles, who gladly believed on the Lord Jesus and were saved. God commissioned His Messiah to be the Light to the Gentiles, and in time, God's plan of redemption would be shared with the Jews by the Gentiles and they would receive salvation.

But now the Gentiles have the light. They have been carrying it in every generation and will continue to do so until our Lord comes again. Then, the Jews will pick up the light and once more offer it to the world. Not only are the Gentiles grafted into Israel, and into her privileges and blessings, but these blessings are represented in the Book of Hebrews as "better" than that which Israel possessed. If Israel is greatly privileged, we are even more privileged.

"God was in Christ, reconciling the world unto Himself," 2Co5:19. Jewish unbelief in Christ frustrated that unstoppable Grace. Because of their choice, of necessity, the progress of the Gospel must not be hindered.

the end result is
ST PAUL'S REVELATION

SAUL OF TARSUS

Saul of Tarsus was born a Jew, "circumcised on the eight day, of the race of Israel, or the tribe of Benjamin, a Hebrew of Hebrew parentage, in observance of the law a Pharisee," Php3:5. The Hebrew name given him by his parents was Saul, but, because his father was a Roman citizen (and therefore Saul inherited Roman citizenship), Saul also had the Latin name St Paul (Acts16:37, 22:25-28), the custom of dual names being common in those days. Since he grew up in a strict Pharisee environment, the name Saul was by far the more appropriate name to go by. But after his conversion Saul determined to bring the Gospel to the Gentiles, so he dusted off his Roman name and became known as St Paul, a name Gentiles were accustomed to.

"Although I am free in regard to all, I have made myself a slave to all so as to win over as many as possible. To the Jews I became a Jew to win over Jews; to those under the Law I became like one under the law - though I myself am not under the law - to win over those under the Law. To those outside the law I became like one outside the law. To the weak I became weak to win over the weak. I have become all things to all, to save at least some. All this I do for the sake of the Gospel, so that I too may have a share in it," 1Co9:19-23.

We can also speculate that this new name is a break with the legacy of his covenant-breaking namesake, as St Paul explained in 1Co9:19-23, 10:33, and Rom15:1. As far as the actual time and place of that name change, this is not clear. It didn't happen at his conversion (Acts 9) and we see the transition made between Saul and St Paul in Acts13:9. After that, St Paul is the name used to refer to him. St Paul must have done it, perhaps reflective of his position as the "least of the apostles" (1Cor9:9), a pun on the meaning of "St Paul" in Greek.

Adopting his Roman name was typical of St Paul's missionary style. His method was to put people at their ease and to approach them with his message in a language and style they could relate to. We should take a clue from St Paul as we engage in apologetics work. No, we don't need to adopt new names, but we should accommodate ourselves to our audiences (and we mean here audiences as small as one person). We want to speak to people in their own styles, so far as we can, and we want to address their particular concerns. We don't want to raise people's hackles before we even have a chance to raise issues.

St Paul was born somewhere between **4 or 5 AD** on the one hand, and probably **15 AD** on the other hand. The first place that St Paul is mentioned is at the martyrdom of St Stephen at the end of Acts 7. He is mentioned there as a young man standing by holding the garments of those who are stoning Stephen. He is called a young man. That is not a technical term. He was probably between the age of eighteen and thirty, we don't really know exactly how old he was at the time but there are some hints that do give us these parameters in Scripture.

It is indicated that based on where he was when he left Jerusalem, when he left Damascus and who was ruling in Damascus that he would have to have left Damascus before 40 AD. Then if Jesus was crucified in 33 AD, and most scholars in chronology place the stoning of Stephen somewhere around 35 AD, and if St Paul is a young man, say eighteen, that would mean that he was born somewhere around 17 AD. If he was twelve years old, then he would have been born somewhere around 5 AD. He came to Jerusalem when he was fourteen to study under Gamaliel (Acts22:3). He would have arrived approximately at the time when Jesus began His public ministry. If he was a little older he would have already been in Jerusalem for may be seven or eight years before Jesus began His public ministry.

It is probably a fair deduction to say that with all the things that were going on around the ministry of Jesus, all of the discussion, John the Baptist's ministry — St Luke tells us that everyone went out to the Jordan to be baptized by John — and when Jesus began to teach the same thing, "Repent for the kingdom of heaven is at hand," there were people saying "Who is He? Is this the Messiah?" These questions were being raised, so it would almost be unrealistic to think that St Paul being in Jerusalem during this time would not have been aware of the presence and the teaching related to Jesus. We can't prove it but it is a fair deduction based on the chronology.

St Paul would probably have had some training already in Tarsus. Tarsus had a university that was highly respected throughout the ancient world. Many scholars believe with varying degrees of certainty that the apostle St Paul was educated there because he demonstrates such a tremendous skill with language and logic and rhetoric that are evidenced within his writing that this would not have all been the result of his rabbinical training but that he had had some education prior to that.

Tarsus was also a major centre for tent making and it is believed that his father probably had a major commercial enterprise in manufacturing tents. St Paul had a Roman citizenship and that would have come through his father. So we can assume that St Paul came from a fairly well-to-do family of merchants who manufactured tents. By the time that St Paul wrote Romans in the winter of 56-57 AD he would be approximately 20 years older, somewhere between 40 and 50 (Acts9:1-19; retold in Acts22:6-21 and Acts26:12-18).

Saul of Tarsus, a Pharisee (Php3:5) in Jerusalem after the crucifixion and resurrection of Jesus Christ, swore to wipe out the new Christian Church, called The Way. He got letters from the high priest, authorizing him to arrest any followers of Jesus in the city of Damascus. On the Damascus Road, Saul and his companions were struck down by a blinding light, brighter than the noonday sun. Saul heard a voice say to him, "Saul, Saul, why do you persecute me?" Acts9:4.

When Saul asked who was speaking to him, the voice replied, "I am Jesus, whom you are persecuting... Now get up and go into the city, and you will be told what you must do," Acts9:5-6. The men with Saul heard the sound but did not see the vision of the risen Christ that Saul did. Saul was blinded. They led him by the hand into Damascus to a man named Judas, on Straight Street. For three days Saul was blind and did not eat or drink anything.

THE CONVERSION OF ST PAUL

Saul's blindness illustrates Christ's teaching on spiritual blindness (Jn9:39). As long as Saul saw things from his own perspective, he is spiritually blind. Only by having his earthly vision taken away does Saul become capable of truly seeing Christ in glory and truth. In one moment of fear, enlightenment, and regret, Saul understood that Jesus was indeed the true Messiah and that he (Saul) had helped murder and imprison innocent people. Saul realized that despite his previous beliefs as a Pharisee, he now knew the truth about God and was obligated to obey him.

Meanwhile, Jesus appeared in a vision to a disciple in Damascus named Ananias and told him to go to Saul. Ananias was afraid because he knew Saul's reputation as a merciless persecutor of the Church. Jesus repeated His command, explaining that Saul was His chosen instrument to deliver the Gospel to the Gentiles, their kings, and the people of Israel (Acts9:15). So, Ananias found Saul at Judas' house, praying for help. Ananias laid his hands on Saul, telling him Jesus had sent him to restore his sight and that Saul might be filled with the Holy Spirit. Something like scales fell from Saul's eyes and he could see again. He arose and was baptised into the Christian faith. Saul ate, regained his strength, and stayed with the Damascus disciples three days.

 The same Jesus Christ who rose from the dead and did such a mighty work in St Paul wants to work in my life too. What could Jesus do if I surrendered as St Paul did and gave Him complete control of my life?

So what did St Paul's conversion involve? First, St Paul had to transcend his narrow constructs, his pre-conditionings and stubborn beliefs by changing his conviction about the ethnic superiority of the Jewish people, with whom alone God made a covenant. For St Paul to accept that God offers his gift of salvation to all peoples, regardless of race, it was necessary to go beyond his thinking that the Jews were ethnically superior to all nations. The Greek word metanoia (translated as 'going beyond the mind') seems to capture the essence of St Paul's conversion experience.

Second, St Paul had to change his idea of the Jewish Messiah. His mental picture of the Messiah was that of a mighty leader who would triumph against Israel's enemies and restore the nation to prosperity and bliss. A crucified Messiah was absurd and inconceivable. St Paul had believed that Jesus was an impostor with false claims to be a Messiah, but the vision on the Damascus Road overturned his notions and expectations about the Messiah. He had to overcome his misconceptions about Jesus of Nazareth and accept Him as truly God's instrument of salvation, not only for Israel but for the rest of the world. This was conversion in its most real sense.

St Paul's experience teaches us that to be Christ's messenger, we need a profound encounter with the Risen Lord. This encounter transforms and makes us accept that we can look foolish in the eyes of the world and wise in the sight of God. St Paul's conversion experience had as its starting point the revelation received from the One he persecuted, a call to us to continually discover who the Risen Lord is for us, as Jesus himself put

St Paul's Revelation

it in his ever relevant question to His disciples: 'But who do you say that I am?' Mk 8:29.

St Paul's experience on the Damascus Road is described in his own letters and in the Acts of the Apostles, in terms of who St Paul was before his conversion and the change that was affected in him. The conversion of Saul shows that Jesus himself wanted the Gospel to go to the Gentiles and that it was no human being's idea. That would quash any argument from the early Jewish Christians that the Gospel was only for the Jews. The men with Saul did not see the risen Jesus, but Saul did. This miraculous message was meant for one person only, Saul.

St Paul's life-changing experience on the Damascus Road led to his baptism and instruction in the Christian faith. He became the most determined of the apostles, suffering brutal physical pain, persecution, and finally martyrdom. He revealed his secret of enduring a lifetime of hardship for the Gospel: "I can do all things through Christ who strengthens me," Php4:13. St Paul knew God called him for a purpose, to explain "the Mystery of Christ" and to be the guardian of God's Grace in the Church, even when other apostles are opposing him. When you read through Galatians you can see his passion for defending

God's Grace; he was not willing to give up one step to the forces of legalism.

The conversion of Saul from zealous persecutor of the Church to the Apostle and indefatigable evangelizer is one of the most important moments in history. It established Christianity as the religion of the New Covenant completely independent of Judaism and not a sect of it.

A man of many talents, St Paul possessed an intimate knowledge of the Hebrew Scriptures. As such, he used the Law, the prophets, and the psalms when he preached to argue that Jesus was the Messiah. St Paul also viewed his own life through the prism of the Sacred Writings, and it was through the Word that he came to understand his own prophetic calling. Upon meeting Jesus face to face on the road to Damascus, he straightaway journeyed into Arabia to meditate on the Scriptures so he could understand the encounter he had had with the Risen One.

ST PAUL A GIFTED EXEGETE AND A PROPHET

Saul of Tarsus possessed perfect qualifications to be an evangelist for Christ: He was versed in Jewish culture and language, his upbringing in Tarsus made him familiar with the Greek language and culture as well, his training in Jewish theology helped him connect the Old Testament with the Gospel, and as a skilled tentmaker he could support himself with that trade.

"For you have heard of my previous way of life in Judaism, how intensely I persecuted the Church of God and tried to destroy it. I was advancing in Judaism beyond many of my own age among my people and was extremely zealous for the traditions of my fathers. But when God, who set me apart from my mother's womb and called me by His Grace, was pleased to reveal his Son in me so that I might preach Him among the Gentiles, my immediate response was not to consult flesh and blood. I did not go up to Jerusalem to see those who were apostles before I was, but I went into Arabia, and then returned to Damascus. Then after three years I went up to Jerusalem," Gal 1:13-17.

The Holy Spirit led St Paul into the desert to prepare him for his ministry as an apostle. And St Paul was more than an apostle — he was a prophet (Gal 1:13-17), like the other great biblical prophets: Moses, Elijah, John the Baptist. They all went through a period of preparation and purification in the wilderness (at the urging of the Spirit) before they began their missions. The Apostle was aware of the divine nature of his calling. In Gal 1:15 he portrays himself to be like the prophet Jeremiah, set apart to preach the word of the Lord before he was conceived. "Before I formed you in the womb I knew you, before you were born I dedicated you, a prophet to the nations I appointed you," Jer1:5.

In the Bible, prophets had the task of faithfully speaking God's Word to the people. They often had both a teaching and revelatory role, declaring God's truth on contemporary issues while also revealing details about the future. Isaiah's ministry, for example, touched on both the present and the future. He preached boldly against the corruption of his day (Is1:4) and delivered grand visions of the future of Israel (Is25:8).

All prophetic teaching is from above, that is, it comes to the prophets by revelation or at least by inspiration. "For prophecy came not by the will of man at any time: but the holy men of God spoke, inspired by the Holy Spirit," 2Pt1:21. Prophets were instrumental in guiding the nation of Israel and establishing the Church. God's household is "built on the foundation of the apostles and prophets, with Christ Jesus Himself as the chief cornerstone," Eph2:20. The office of the prophets in the New Testament Church was to explain infallibly the true meaning of the ancient prophecies, and also themselves to predict future events, by virtue of the extraordinary revelations made to them.

St Paul was more than a prophet. His calling by the Lord ordained him to be a missionary to the new people of God. St Paul received religious instruction directly from Jesus, the source of love and life Himself. Now he had only to pay his debt to Christ, to pass on the faith to everyone he met. He didn't do this out of fear but out of obligation and out of love. "If I preach the Gospel, this is no reason for me to boast, for an obligation has been imposed on me, and woe to me if I do not preach it!" 1Co9:16.

St Paul felt he was "less than the least of all believers" (Eph3:8) as he could never forget what he was doing before Christ, which is exactly why he was chosen by God. He also understood how great a privilege it was to be chosen to be the messenger of God's great mystery in Christ. The Gospel that he preached was revealed to him by Jesus Christ (Gal 1:11).

Returning from Arabia, St Paul was thinking: What should I do? Return to my former life in Judaism, as a Pharisee and respected religious leader? Or should I go into the religious houses of study and worship and proclaim that Jesus is the Son of God? I could go back to the High Priest in Jerusalem and work things out. I have committed no unforgiveable offense, did not break the Law. I got ambushed out there on the road and sidetracked in my mission to arrest these men and women who follow the Way. Caiaphas and Ananias will understand. What should I do?

The Acts of the Apostles reports St Paul's answer to the great question on his mind: "He began at once to proclaim Jesus in the synagogues, that he is the Son of God," Acts9:20. What is God promising me? A life of persecution and mistreatment, of tireless preaching, peril, and temporal hungers, humiliation and persecution: How can I refuse? St Paul's answer to his calling, his very own fiat, became the basis for the New Testament, the fundamental theology on which the entire Church has been constructed. When he returned from Arabia to Damascus, he stepped across the threshold of the synagogue in Damascus to preach Christ crucified and risen. In that instance, St Paul straddled his past and his future, even the fate of the world.

"But when (God), who from my mother's womb had set me apart and called me through His Grace, was pleased to reveal His Son to me, so that I might proclaim Him to the Gentiles, I did not immediately consult flesh and blood, nor did I go up to Jerusalem to those who were apostles before me; rather, I went into Arabia, and then returned to Damascus. Then after three years I went up to Jerusalem," Gal 1:17-18.

St Paul describes his call in "prophetic" terms: "the God who set me apart from my mother's womb . . ." (Gal 1:15; Is49:1; Jer1:5). Even though the Hebrew scriptures are silent about Elijah's birth or call, this locates St Paul firmly within the prophetic tradition of which Elijah was one of the supreme members. Whatever still, small voice he may have heard, it was certainly not underwriting the land of zeal in which he had been indulging up until then. His zeal was now to be redirected (Gal 4:18; 2Co11:2). He was to become the herald of the new king. At this point, of course, the parallel with Elijah suddenly ceases to be exact. Saul of Tarsus was being told, through his whole Damascus Road Encounter with Our Lord Jesus Christ, that the way of zeal was not the way by which the eschatological mission was to be accomplished.

Nevertheless, a parallel still holds. Elijah was sent with a message to anoint Hazael king of Syria and Jehu king of Israel; they, and Elijah's own successor Elisha, would complete the work that Elijah's zeal had begun. Saul was sent back from Arabia to be the herald of the newly anointed Messiah, Jesus (Gal 1:16, 23). His was the kingship that would challenge all pagan powers (Gal 4:1-11), that would create the true community of the people of God. St Paul may here be indicating that he had exchanged the role of Elijah-like zeal for the role of the servant. Instead of inflicting the wrath of YHWH on rebellious Jews, he would become the light of the nations. He now had a new role model, a new job description.

The Christian St Paul's verdict on the pre-Christian Saul is this: He had a zeal for Israel's God, but it was an ignorant zeal, seeking to establish a covenant membership for Jews and Jews only, and to see that identity marked out by the works of Torah. What Saul learned on the road to Damascus, and perhaps on Sinai too as he reflected on Elijah's post-zeal humiliation, was that the true remnant was a remnant defined by the divine call, not by works.

St Paul's conclusion: "But the God of Israel called me, like Elijah, to step back from this zeal and to listen to Him afresh. When I listened, I heard a voice telling me that the messianic victory over evil had already been won, and that I and my fellow Jewish Christians were the true remnant, saved by Grace and marked out by faith, apart from ethnic identity and works of Torah. I therefore had to renounce my former zeal, and announce the true Messiah to the world."

The cross offered the solution to the problem that "zeal" had sought to address. The revelation of the crucified, and now risen, Messiah was therefore sufficient to stop the zealous Saul in his tracks, to send him back like his role model to Sinai, and to convince him that the battle he was blindly fighting had already been won, and indeed that by fighting it he had been losing it.

THE MYSTERY OF CHRIST

St Paul's Revelation

St Paul writes to the Ephesians about his "insight into the Mystery of Christ," Eph3:4. The "mystery" expresses the essence of the Gospel - the good news of Jesus Christ.

"When you read this you can perceive my insight into the Mystery of Christ, which was not made known to the sons of men in other generations as it has now been revealed to His holy apostles and prophets by the Spirit; that is, how the Gentiles are fellow heirs, members of the same body, and partakers of the promise in Christ Jesus through the Gospel," Eph3:4-6.

"Mystery" is not to be understood as "mysterious" (as is the case with mystical ecstasies, vibrations, the occult, or hobgoblins).

Mystery and superstition have nothing in common. People love the magical, the bizarre, and the sensational. We are more interested in teasing our curiosity than understanding the truth. God gives us the right kind of mystery in the Gospel message. The simple and divine things always have a mystery to them such as marriage (Eph5:20-33).

"Mystery" is not the absence of meaning, but it is the presence of a greater meaning than we can comprehend. The fact that you cannot fully understand something does not mean that you cannot understand it at all. No one can fully grasp love, faith, justice, or goodness; but we believe in them and seek to exhibit them.

A mystery defies our grasp and is difficult to communicate. Eternal principles are larger than human words. Mystery is understood only by revelation, not by reason. God can be known but not figured out. We cannot understand God's Grace until we accept His wrath. Until we understand the Cross, we cannot understand Christianity. We do not conquer mystery — we use it, grow in it, and celebrate it.

Mystery requires obedience without full knowledge. We are simply to trust and obey the plain truths of the Scriptures and grow in the knowledge of the Word every day! We must know enough not to deny what we cannot understand.

The Gospel of Christ was revealed through the prophetic writings, that is, the Old Testament Scriptures. The gospel St Paul preached was "according to the (Old Testament) Scriptures" (1Co15:3-4)! His basic themes of the Cross and the empty tomb and justification by faith were themes that could be found in the Old Testament. There was no mystery is this.

Today there is a "mystery" aspect of the Gospel which was unknown in other ages but which now forms the very core of the Gospel preaching of this age: "Which in other ages was not made known unto the sons of men, as it is now revealed unto His holy apostles and prophets by the Spirit," Eph3:5. When it came to mystery truth, the Old Testament prophets were totally in the dark. The only One who knew about the mysteries in the Old Testament period was God Himself. The reference here is to New Testament apostles and prophets (1Co12:10, 29; Eph2:20; Eph4:11). The mysteries of God are revealed in all the fullness of their preciousness in St Paul's letters, but the apostle Paul was not the first to reveal these secrets. This mystery, once kept secret, is now revealed! It is a secret no longer! That which was hidden is now being made known!

Thus, by definition, the New Testament mystery is that which was hidden, kept secret, and not made known to men in previous generations (prior to St Paul's generation) but was made manifest and revealed in the New Testament era to and by the New Testament apostles and prophets.

The distinctive element of Gospel preaching in this Church Age: The idea that Gentiles should be on exactly the same plane as Israelites and, furthermore, in the intimate relationship as being members of the same body, is absolutely foreign to the Old Testament. According to Is61:5-6, the Gentiles are pictured as being the servants and Israel as the priests of God. While it is true that the Gentiles were promised blessings in the future millennial kingdom, they are never given equality with the Jews in the Old Testament.

The Old Testament does predict Gentile blessing for the millennial period (Is61:5-6; 2:1-4), but the blessings do not include equality with the Jews as is true today in the Body of Christ. Great blessing is promised Gentiles in the predictions of the Old Testament, but not on the basis of equality of position with the Jews. This equality is the point of the mystery revealed to the apostles and prophets in New Testament times that the Gentiles should be fellow heirs, and of the same body, and partakers of His promise in Christ by the Gospel

There are seven aspects of "the Mystery of Christ" that are mentioned by the apostle Paul in his Letters to the saints: The first mystery is the mystery of the Incarnation

(1Ti3:16). The second mystery revealed to the apostle St Paul is the mystery of the Indwelling Christ (Col 1:25-28). The third mystery is the mystery of the Church (Eph3:1-10). The fourth mystery is the mystery of the blindness of Israel (Rom11:25-26). The fifth mystery is the mystery of the Translation of the Church (1 Co15:50-58). The sixth mystery is the revelation of the antichrist — the mystery of iniquity (2Th2:1-9). The seventh mystery is the mystery of the Bride of Christ (Eph5:22-32).

Thus, for each aspect of the mystery, we find either a quotation from, or a reference to, the Old Testament Scriptures. However, there is a mystery aspect of the Gospel which was unknown in other ages but which now forms the very core of the Gospel preaching of this age: "that the Gentiles should be fellow heirs, and of the same body, and partakers of His promise in Christ by the Gospel," Eph3:6. This new revelation was previously unknown.

It should be noted that mystery truth had been revealed, at least in germ form, by our Lord Jesus Christ. This is seen especially in the mysteries of Matthew 13 and in the Upper Room Discourse of John 14-17. Here are some examples:

- The mystery of the church was anticipated in

Mt13:45-46.

- The mystery of "Christ in you" (Col 1:27) was anticipated in Jn14:20 and 17:23.
- The mystery of the oneness of Christ and His church (Eph5:31-32) was anticipated in Jn17:21-23.
- The mystery of the rapture (1Co15:51-52) was anticipated in Jn14:1-3.
- The mystery of the present status of the nation Israel (Rom11:25) was anticipated in Mt13:44.
- The mystery of iniquity working throughout the course of this present age (2Th2:9) was anticipated in the parables of the mustard seed and leaven.
- The mystery of Jews and Gentiles being united together in one body (Eph3:5-6) was anticipated in Jn10:16.

THE MYSTERY OF
THE INCARNATION

 "And without controversy great is the mystery of godliness: God was manifested in the flesh, justified in the Spirit, seen by angels, preached among the Gentiles, believed on in the world, received up in glory," 1Ti 3:16.

HYMN OF FAITH

In this verse, we are looking at a first-century confession of faith that many believe was sung as a hymn in the early New Testament Church. St Paul begins with the statement "And without controversy great is the mystery of godliness." Undeniably, the truth which the Apostle was about to state, admitted of no dispute.

"Great" means of supreme importance and significance. The mystery of godliness is great, not because it is a riddle and cannot be known, but because it is hidden to the natural man and known only to believing hearts. There are mysteries in the life of Christ that are to be believed, even though they cannot be explained. The finite mind cannot fathom the mystery of godliness. Indeed, great is the mystery of godliness!

The mystery of godliness, which is the pillar and ground of the truth, is, without controversy, a great thing. The meaning of "mystery" here is not that the proposition which he affirms was mysterious in the sense that it was unintelligible, or impossible to be understood; but that the doctrine respecting the incarnation and the work of the Messiah, which had been so long "kept hidden" from the world, was a subject of the deepest importance. This passage, therefore, should not be used to prove that there is anything unintelligible, or anything that surpasses human comprehension, in that doctrine, whatever may be the truth on that point; but that the doctrine which he now proceeds to state, and which had been so long concealed from mankind, was of the utmost consequence.

Then St Paul proceeds to show what this mystery of godliness is; he sums it up in the following six particulars:

1. God was manifest in the flesh

"In the flesh" refers to the Incarnation of Jesus Christ. This is a direct reference to the deity of Jesus. "He was revealed in the flesh." Jesus was God manifest in the flesh (Jn1:1 and 14). This means Jesus became a human being. He ate, slept, bled, and died as any other human does. This is the essence of the incarnation; that God the

Son, the Second Person of the Holy Trinity, added to His deity humanity - and was thus manifested in the flesh.

 St John Chrysostom: And wonder not that St Paul says in another place, "God was manifested in the Flesh", because the manifestation took place by means of the flesh, not according to (His) Essence. Besides, St Paul shows that He is invisible, not only to men, but also to the powers above, for after saying, "was manifested in the Flesh," he adds, "was seen of angels."

2. Justified in the Spirit

We can say that Jesus was justified by the Spirit not in the sense that He was once sinful but made righteous, but in the sense that He was declared to be, by the Holy Spirit, what He always was - completely justified before the Father. When Jesus came to this earth, He did not come as a mighty King, revealing the splendour of God. He took the lowly form of a servant. Thus the ministry of the Holy Spirit was to declare Jesus to be the Righteous One by attesting to His deity.

Jesus was declared righteous through the power of the Holy Spirit as evidenced by His works and miracles: "No man can do these miracles...except God be with him" (Jn3:2). The Saviour cast out devils by Him (Mt12:28); the Spirit was given to him without measure (Jn3:34).

All the manifestations of God to Him; all the power of working miracles by His agency; all the influences imparted to the man Christ Jesus, endowing Him with such wisdom as man never had before, may be regarded as an attestation of the Holy Spirit to the divine mission of the Lord Jesus, and of course as a vindication from all the charges against Him. Jesus said, "Which of you convicts Me of sin?" (Jn8:46). 1Pt2:22 states, "He committed no sin, and no deceit was found in his mouth." He was "holy, harmless, undefiled, separate from sinners" (Heb7:26). Had He not been what He professed to be, God would not have borne such a decisive testimony to His Messiahship.

The Holy Spirit furnished the evidence that He was the Son of God, or "justified" His claims. When Jesus identified Himself with sinners by submitting to baptism, the Spirit "justified" Him by descending on Him as a dove (Mt3:16). When He went to the extreme humiliation of the cross and bore our sin, being numbered with the transgressors, the

Holy Spirit declared Jesus to be the Son of God by raising Him from the dead (Rom1:4). If Jesus had been a sinner, then He would have had to die for His own sins, and God would not have raised Him from the dead. But the fact that God did raise Jesus from the dead proves that He is the Righteous One. Christ was, justified from all the calumnies of the Jews, who crucified Him as an impostor.

All these miracles, being wrought by the power of God, were a full proof of His innocence. Thus, the Spirit was sent to convince the world of sin because it did not believe on Him (Jn16:8-9); and He was sent down in accordance with His promise, to convert the hearts of people (Acts2:33). In like manner, the descent of the Holy Spirit on the day of Pentecost, and His agency in the conversion of every sinner, prove the same thing, and furnish the grand argument in vindication of the Redeemer that He was sent from God.

To this the apostle refers as a part of the glorious truth of the Christian scheme now revealed - the "mystery of religion"; as a portion of the amazing records, the memory of which the Church was to preserve as connected with the redemption of the world.

The Mystery Of The Incarnation

3. Seen of angels

Angels had an interest in the Saviour from His conception to His ascension. An angel announced the conception to St Mary (Lk1:30-38; Mt1:20-25), angels proclaimed His birth to the shepherds(Lk2:9-11), angels ministered to Him after His temptation in the wilderness (Mt4:11), an angel strengthened Him in His agony in the Garden of Gethsemane (Lk22:43), angels proclaimed His resurrection at the tomb (Lk24:4-5), and angels addressed the disciples at Christ's ascension (Acts1:10). Perhaps here the reference is especially to Christ's resurrection, which secured God's ultimate victory over Satan and his demonic hosts.

Before our Lord's ascension to heaven, these holy beings could have little knowledge of the necessity, reasons, and economy of human salvation; nor of the nature of Christ as God and man. St Peter informs us that the angels desire to look into these things (1Pt1:12). And St Paul says the same thing (Eph3:9-10), when speaking of the revelation of the Gospel plan of salvation, which he calls the mystery. From the Beginning of the World, the mystery which had been hidden in God, was now published, that unto the Principalities and Powers in heavenly places might be Made Known, by the Church, the manifold wisdom of God. Even those angelic beings have got an accession to their blessedness, by an increase of knowledge in the things which concern Jesus Christ, and the whole scheme of human salvation, through His incarnation, passion, death, resurrection, ascension, and glorification.

The design of the apostle is to give an impressive view of the grandeur and glory of that work which attracted the attention of the heavenly hosts, and which drew them from the skies that they might proclaim His advent, sustain Him in His temptations, witness His crucifixion, and watch over Him in the tomb. The work of Christ, though despised by people, excited the deepest interest in heaven (1Pt1:12).

4. Preached unto the Gentiles

This is another way of saying the nations. After the resurrection, the Lord Jesus made it plain to the disciples that the message of salvation was not just for the Jews, but for all nations: "Go therefore and make disciples of all the nations, baptizing them in the name of the Father and the Son and the Holy Spirit, teaching them to observe all that I commanded you," Mt28:19-20. God's way of creating faith in men's hearts is not by pictures, music, or symbols, but by the hearing of the Word of God.

There is only one message for every people, that "Christ died for our sins according to the Scriptures, and that He was buried, and that He was raised on the third day according to the Scriptures" (1Co15:3-4). "And this gospel of the kingdom shall be preached in all the world for a witness unto all nations; and then shall the end come," Mt24:14. This was one grand part of the mystery which had been hidden in God, that the Gentiles should be made fellow heirs with the Jews, and be admitted into the Kingdom of God.

Before His coming, a wall of partition had divided the Jewish and Gentile world. The Jews regarded the rest of mankind as excluded from the covenant mercies of God, and it was one of the principal stumbling blocks in their way, in regard to the Gospel, that it proclaimed that all the race was on a level, that that middle wall of partition was broken down, and that salvation might now be published to all people (Acts22:21; Eph2:14-15; Rom3:22; Rom10:11-20). To the Gentiles, therefore, He was proclaimed as having pulled down the middle wall of partition between them and the Jews; that, through Him, God had granted unto them repentance unto life; and that they also might have redemption in His blood, the forgiveness of sins.

5. Believed on in the world

This is the only means that God has ordained for every person around the world to receive the gift of eternal life: "God so loved the world that He gave His only begotten Son that whoever believes in Him should not perish, but have eternal life" (Jn3:16). Everywhere that Christ is preached, faith comes (Rom10:17) and new believers are added to the body of Christ. Jesus was received by mankind as the promised Messiah, the Anointed of God, and the only Saviour of fallen man. This is a most striking part of the mystery of godliness, that one who was crucified as a malefactor, and whose kingdom is not of this world, and whose doctrines are opposed to all the sinful propensities of the human heart, should, wherever His Gospel is preached, be acknowledged as the only Saviour of sinners, and the Judge of the living and dead! Notwithstanding their prejudices, many even of the Jews believed on Him; and a great company of the priests themselves, who were his crucifiers, became obedient to the faith (Acts6:7). This was an additional proof of Christ's innocence.

6. Received up into Glory

This refers to Jesus' ascension back into heaven after His resurrection (Acts1:9-11). Christ's ascension testified that the Father had accepted His redeeming work fully, His finished work on our behalf (Heb1:3), and His present intercession for us (1Jn2:1). Jesus ascended into heaven in a resurrection body; yet it was a body that still retained the marks of His great work of love for us. It still had the nail prints in His hands and feet, the wound in his side, all marks of His suffering on our behalf (Jn20:24-29).

It also means that not only Jesus but more will be taken up into heaven with Him. St Paul's description of Jesus after the passage speaking of Christian character reminds us of the key to our own character transformation - beholding Jesus. It is just as St Paul wrote in 2Co3:18: "But we all, with unveiled face, beholding as in a mirror the glory of the Lord, are being transformed into the same image from glory to glory, just as by the Spirit of the Lord." Jesus is the perfect fulfilment of these descriptions of Christian character.

Now Jesus is seated at the right hand of the Father, with all authority in heaven and earth. As the angels promised, one day He will return to earth in the same manner as He ascended: visibly, bodily, in power and glory.

"And without controversy great is the mystery of godliness: God was manifested in the flesh, justified in the Spirit, seen by angels, preached among the Gentiles, believed on in the world, received up in glory,"1Ti3:16.

This hymn speaks of the Incarnation (birth) of Jesus Christ at Bethlehem: His life, teachings, death, and resurrection, which fully reveal the Father (Jn1:14-18). There is also the strong inference of His pre-existence (Jn1:1-5; 8:57-58; 2Co8:4; Php2:6; Col 1:17). This is the central truth of the Gospels about Jesus Christ, that He was fully God and fully human (Jn1:14; Php2:6-8; Col 1:14-16; 1Jn4:1-6). Thus this verse packs a lot of theology in a nutshell: the incarnation, life, death, resurrection, commission, and ascension of the Lord Jesus Christ. He is God revealed in human flesh, and, as such, is the only Saviour.

The first point is, Jesus is God was manifested in the flesh; the last, He was taken up into glory. This "mystery", which had "been hidden from ages and from generations, and which was now manifest" (Col 1:26), was the great doctrine on which depended "religion" everywhere, or was that which constituted the Christian scheme. It was specified in six points, which sum up the whole economy of Christ upon earth. It is the pillar and ground, the foundation and support of all the truth taught in His Church.

We trust that Jesus will transform our life according to the same character, as we put our focus on Him. We sometimes want religion to build this character in us; but truly, relationship with Jesus is what really does it.

Great is the mystery of godliness. There are mysteries in the life of Christ that are to be believed, even though they cannot be explained. The finite mind cannot fathom the mystery of godliness. The doctrine of the Incarnation is distinct and unique to the Christian faith. Many religions speak of appearances of deities in the guise of men or animals. But these are 'appearances' only. None takes the startling position of Christianity, which affirms that the God who existed from eternity and who created all things entered His creation to actually become a human being. Yet this is just the radical affirmation of the Christian faith.

The work of redemption is called a mystery, and it is indeed the mystery by which everlasting righteousness is brought to all who believe. The race in consequence of sin was at enmity with God. Christ, at an infinite cost, by a painful process, mysterious to angels as well as to men, assumed humanity (1Pt1:11-12). Hiding His divinity, laying aside His glory, He was born a babe in Bethlehem. In human flesh, He lived the Law of God, that He might condemn sin in the flesh, and bear witness to heavenly intelligences that the Law was ordained to life and to ensure the happiness, peace, and eternal good of all who obey. But the same infinite sacrifice that is life to those who believe is a testimony of condemnation to the disobedient, speaking death and not life.

Thus, St Paul taught that Jesus is the divine pre-existent Son of God who became man in order to redeem His people from their sins in order that they might escape from the wrath to come. The hymn of 1Ti3:16 must therefore be understood in light of this background.

THE MYSTERY OF
THE INDWELLING CHRIST

"(The Church) of which I became a minister according to the stewardship from God which was given to me for you, to fulfil the Word of God, the mystery which has been hidden from ages and from generations, but now has been revealed to His saints. To them God willed to make known what are the riches of the glory of this mystery among the Gentiles: which is Christ in you, the hope of glory. Him we preach, warning every man and teaching every man in all wisdom, that we may present every man perfect in Christ Jesus," Col 1:25-28.

God has a mystery. God's mystery is God's secret masterplan for the universe. That cosmic masterplan, God's will and purpose, has been kept secret for centuries, but it has now been revealed in Jesus Christ. What a wonderful and glorious mystery it is. And the secret is simply this. "Christ in you – the hope of glory." This mystery is what godliness is all about. St Paul told us that the secret is none other than Christ Himself indwelling us (Col 1:27). It is not a philosophy or a religion; rather, it is a Person – Jesus Christ our Lord living in our hearts. We

have the happy certainty that one day we will share God's glory. And our guarantee of heaven is in God's masterplan – "Christ in you!

What is a Christian? In Col 1:27 St Paul makes this very clear. "Christ in you." A Christian is somebody in whom Jesus Christ is alive and at work. "I have been crucified with Christ and I no longer live, but Christ lives in me. The life I live in the body, I live by faith in the Son of God, who loved me and gave Himself for me," Gal 2: 20.

Jesus Christ is the image of God, the exact likeness of God, the perfect human representation of the Almighty, All-knowing, Ever-present, Eternal, Holy, Ever-Loving, Transcendent God. Christ is the image of God – and Christ is in us!

Jesus Christ is the firstborn of God, the Creator and Sustainer of everything that exists, standing first in line in this present age. And Jesus Christ is the firstborn of the age to come, the first to rise from the dead in God's new creation, the Church. Christ is the firstborn of God – and Christ is in us! Jesus Christ is the fullness of God – and Christ is in us!

One of the greatest differences between New Testament believers and Old Testament believers is the fact that New Testament believers are the temple of God. God Himself actually indwells them. In the Old Testament, the Spirit of God would come upon people and anoint them for service. He even came within Old Testament prophets to inspire them to write the scriptures, but this was temporary.

Now, in the days of the New Testament, God lives in the hearts of those who make Jesus their Lord (Rom10:9). The believer's spirit has become the temple of God. The New Testament is clear that Christ, by the Holy Spirit, takes up permanent residence in all believers (Eph2:22; 2Co5:17). "But you are not in the flesh but in the Spirit, if indeed the Spirit of God dwells in you. Now if anyone does not have the Spirit of Christ, he is not His," Rom8:9. "And what agreement has the temple of God with idols? For you are the temple of the living God. As God has said: 'I will dwell in them and walk among them. I will be their God, and they shall be My people'," 2Co6:16. Our responsibility is to present our bodies as members of righteousness unto and in union with Him. "And do not present your members as instruments of unrighteousness to sin, but present yourselves to God as being alive from the dead, and your members as instruments of righteousness to God," Rom6:13.

Christ is in the believer. He indwells the heart by faith, as the sun indwells the lowliest flowers that unfurl their petals and bare their hearts to its beams. Not because we are good. Not because we are trying to be wholehearted in our consecration. Not because we keep Him by the tenacity of our love. But because we believe, and in believing, have thrown open all the doors and windows of our nature. And He has come in.

It is very wonderful. Yes; the heavens, even the Heavens of heavens, with all their light and glory, alone seem worthy of Him. But even there He is not more at home than He is with the humble and contrite spirit that simply trusts in Him. In His early life, He said that the Father dwelt in Him so that the words He spoke and the works He did were not His own, but His Father's. And He desires to be in us as His Father was in Him, so that the outgoings of our life may be channels through which He, hidden within, may pour Himself forth upon men.

SIGNIFICANCE OF "CHRIST IN YOU"

Christ in you accepted by faith alone means Christ possessed. When Christ is in you the Law has nothing more to say to you. It can no longer condemn you because God has declared you acquitted. You have been justified by faith in Christ.

Christ in you means Christ experienced in all His power. Christ in you fills your life with His holy presence and power. That which the law can never do, Christ does by indwelling in you.

Christ in you is His sovereign rule in your life. Christ in you is Christ's sceptre from the centre of your being over every facet of your personality. Christ in you is His power bringing every thought into captivity to Himself. Christ in you means the imperial sovereignty of Jesus Christ over your life. We find our freedom by being in submission to His sovereign hand over our lives.

Christ in you means His filling you with His wonderful presence. Christ in you transforms your person until you become like Christ.

Christ in me means that He is bearing me along from within. His motive-power carries me on giving my whole life a wonderful sense of God's presence. It gives me life with an endless song in my heart.

When Christ enters into our lives and we yield to His Presence. He transforms, elevates us to His likeness. The apostle St Paul declared, I live, yet not I, Christ lives in me. When Christ enters in He sanctifies us, and sets us apart for His glory.

Christ in you means He enters into us and becomes our life. Christ in you means His power in you. We were without spiritual strength until Christ came into our lives. We were dead in trespasses and sins. Now our spiritual victory is guaranteed.

Christ in you means we are spiritually rich. We were in spiritual poverty until Christ came in and now we have all the riches of Christ Jesus. We are now rich because He is rich.

Christ in you means honour and glory. He glorifies the place where He dwells even for a moment. If Christ comes into your heart His whole court comes with Him! Rejoice for you have Him as a holy guest. People who value and love Him cannot be happy without Him.

"CHRIST IN YOU" IN THE SACRAMENTS

In the New Testament, the mystery of "Christ in you" is experienced in the sacraments of the Church which are called the "mysteries". The Lord indwells people through the new birth (Sacrament of Baptism), and they become His permanent abode (Jn14:16). The believer's spirit has become the temple of God. The Holy Spirit indwells the regenerated believers in the Sacrament of Chrismation. "Or do you not know that your body is the temple of the Holy Spirit who is in you, whom you have from God, and you are not your own? For you were bought at a price; therefore, glorify God in your body and in your spirit, which are God's." 1Co6:19-20. Eating His flesh, and drinking His blood in the Sacrament of the Holy Eucharist is the means or instrument by which men receive Him into their hearts, and retain Him, and have communion with Him (Jn6:53-56).

"Most assuredly, I say to you, unless you eat the flesh of the Son of Man and drink His blood, you have no life in you. Whoever eats My flesh and drinks My blood has eternal life, and I will raise him up at the last day. For My flesh is food indeed, and My blood is drink indeed. He who eats My flesh and drinks My blood abides in Me, and I in him," Jn6:53-56.

The Mystery Of The Indwelling Christ

St Cyril of Jerusalem: Jesus Christ, by His will, once changed water into wine at Cana of Galilee. So why should we not believe that He can change wine into blood? We should therefore have full assurance that we are sharing in the body and blood of Christ. For in the form of bread, His body is given to you, and in the form of wine, His blood is given to you, so that by partaking of the body and blood of Christ you may become of one body and one blood with Him.

St John of Damascus: And now you ask how the bread becomes the body of Christ, and the wine and the water become the blood of Christ. I shall tell you. The Holy Spirit comes upon them, and achieves things which surpass every word and thought.... Let it be enough for you to understand that this takes place by the Holy Spirit.

In Communion, we truly eat His flesh and drink His blood and this grants the faithful eternal life. He dwells in believers, not in such sense as He dwells in the world, by His omnipresence, and power; or in the human nature,

by hypostatical union to it; but by His Spirit, and by faith, which is an instance of wonderful condescending Grace. It is owing to union to Him, and is expressive of communion with Him, and is what will continue for ever.

Most of us are aware of the vertical dimension of the Eucharist, of the fact that it unites us to God as His people. "He who eats my flesh and drinks my blood abides in Me and I in him," said Jesus. It is this Sacrament which makes it possible for us to say with St Paul, "Christ lives in me". And through this Sacrament, we can leave the Lord's Table with the glowing courage of the same St Paul who said, "I can do all things through Christ who strengthens me".

Few Christians, however, realize the horizontal dimension of the Eucharist, the fact that it unites us not only to God, but also to each other. Through the Eucharist we all become one in Christ since the same Christ comes to dwell in all of us. The Fathers of the Church take for granted the unity of the individual to God through the Eucharist. What they stress and emphasize greatly is the horizontal dimension of Communion, our becoming one with each other in Christ. The very fact that we all share the one Bread makes us one Body, explains St Paul.

Jesus Christ tells us that the first and greatest commandment is love of God and man. Yet we all know from experience that it is not always easy to love our fellow men. God knew that this was a difficult commandment. That is why He gave us the Sacrament of Communion through which He gives us His own strength to enable us to practice this commandment of love.

Orthodoxy is the religion of love especially because it believes that through the Eucharist, Christ comes to live in us thus making us all a community of brothers and sisters. This is why the liturgy in our Church is never celebrated in private, just by the priest alone, but always with the family of God, the congregation, present. This is done in order to express the horizontal dimension of the Eucharist, i.e., the fact that by receiving the Body and Blood of Christ we are all joined together in one body, one family, the family of God.

This means that the same Christ who comes to us in Holy Communion comes to us also in the person of our neighbour, our fellow parishioner, our fellow Christian: Christ lives in every person I meet. "For as much as you did it unto one of these the least of my brethren you did it to me," said Jesus. The way I treat my fellow men is the way I treat Christ. To honour Christ in the Sacrament of Communion and to dis-honour Him in the person of my fellow men is sacrilege, sin and hypocrisy.

The Lord's commitment to indwell us and never leave us or forsake us (Heb13:5) must be taken as an indication of His great love for us. If we continually thought upon this with all its implications, how could we ever be lonely or discouraged? We couldn't! Depression and self-pity would cease! What would it matter what others think of us if we truly understand how much Jesus thinks of us?

Our attitudes and fears reveal that this revelation of "Christ in us" is not a well-established fact in most Christians. However, this verse makes it clear that our Father wants to make "the riches of the glory of this mystery" known unto us. We should all be seeking a greater revelation of this truth. St Paul was saying that Christ in us is a taste and guarantee of what is to come. If we had a real revelation of the reality of Christ in us (Col 1:27), it would drastically change our attitudes, emotions, and actions.

One of the ministries of the Holy Spirit is to bring back to our remembrance things that Jesus has spoken unto us.

"But the Helper, the Holy Spirit, whom the Father will send in My name, He will teach you all things, and bring to your remembrance all things that I said to you," Jn14:26. Four times Jesus emphasized the Holy Spirit as being the one to reveal the truths of God to the believer. In this instance, Jesus said the Holy Spirit would guide us into all truth. During this same night, Jesus said, "Thy word is truth" (Jn17:17). Therefore, the Holy Spirit is specifically given to give revelation knowledge of God's Word (Lk2:26, Jn6:45, Jn7:15). A guide doesn't do everything for us but rather leads us. The Holy Spirit will lead us into all truth, but we have to follow. We have to go to the effort of studying, trusting that the Holy Spirit is leading us. "Jesus answered and said to him, 'If anyone loves Me, he will keep My word; and My Father will love him, and We will come to him and make Our home with him'," Jn14:23.

To dwell or abide in Him is to remain in the belief of His doctrine, and in the participation of the benefits of His death. We partake of Christ and His benefits by faith. The soul that rightly knows its state and wants, finds whatever can calm the conscience, and promote true holiness, in the redeemer, God manifest in the flesh. Meditating upon the Cross of Christ gives life to our repentance, love, and gratitude. We live by Him, as our bodies live by our food. We live by Him, as the members by the head, the branches by the root: because He lives we shall live also.

Jesus dwells in believers by His Spirit and doctrine. When His Spirit is given them to sanctify them; when His temper, His meekness, His humility, and His love pervade their hearts; when His doctrine is received by them and influences their life, and when they are supported by the consolations of the Gospel, it may be said that He abides or dwells in them. The saints are the habitation or dwelling place of Christ; He dwells not in their heads and to tongues, but in their hearts by faith.

Catherine of Siena at one time spent three days in a solitary retreat, praying for a greater fullness and joy of the Divine presence. Instead of this, it seemed as though legions of wicked spirits assailed her with blasphemous thoughts and evil suggestions. At length, a great light appeared to descend from above. The devils fled, and the Lord Jesus conversed with her. Catherine asked Him: "Lord, where were You when my heart was so tormented?"

"I was in your heart," He answered.

"O Lord, You are everlasting truth," she replied, "and I humbly bow before Your word, but how can I believe that You were in my heart when it was filled with such detestable thoughts?"

"Did these thoughts give you pleasure or pain?" He asked.

"An exceeding pain and sadness", was her reply.

To whom the Lord said, "You were in woe and sadness because I was in the midst of your heart. It was My presence which rendered those thoughts insupportable to you. When the period I had determined for the duration of the combat had elapsed, I sent forth the beams of My light, and the shades of hell were dispelled, because they cannot resist that light."

It is the personal experience of the living presence of Christ in the individual life of the believer that is the mystery

of mysteries. This is a wonderful truth that some fail to fully appreciate. Solomon said at the dedication of the temple, "But will God indeed dwell on the earth? Behold, heaven and the heaven of heavens cannot contain You. How much less this temple which I have built! 1Kg8:27. We could say, "How much less this physical body?" This is truly amazing!

The central fact of an intimate personal relationship with Christ is this great truth of Christ in you. This indwelling constitutes the hope of glory for every believer. Jesus is the Shekinah glory of God, and He shines in our hearts so that we see the glory of God in the face of Christ (2Co3:18; 4:6, 16; 1 Jn3:2-3). Whatever Christ is His people are in Him. They are crucified in Him, they were dead in Him, they were buried in Him, they were risen in Him; in Him they live eternally, in Him they sit gloriously at the right hand of God, who has raised us up together, and made us sit together in the heavenly places in Christ Jesus. In Him we are accepted in the beloved, both now and forever.

The ministry of the Holy Spirit is available to all believers who have been baptised by the water and the Spirit (Sacrament of Baptism) and have received the Holy Spirit (Sacrament of Chrismation), but it is not operable in all Spirit-filled believers. It must be appropriated by faith.

Anything short of Jesus Christ will leave you short of salvation. You have to reach Christ, and touch Christ and nothing short of this will save you. Jesus gives us Himself. To have Christ is to have eternal life. He does not merely give us wisdom, righteousness, sanctification, redemption etc. He is our life. Therefore, we cannot do without Him.

Christ in us – that is our starting point. From there we press on to Christian maturity. That is St Paul's goal for every Christian. "Him we preach, warning every man and teaching every man in all wisdom, that we may present every man perfect in Christ Jesus," Col 1:28.

We have Christ inside already – transforming us into His image until we reach perfection, or maturity, in Christ. "And we, who with unveiled faces all reflect the Lord's glory, are being transformed into His likeness with ever-increasing glory, which comes from the Lord, who is the Spirit," 2Co3:18.

The Spirit of God is at work in us, transforming us into the likeness of Christ. This isn't about having more of Christ in us. We already have all of Christ in us. We already have all the resources we could ever need to live the Christian life. What we need is "Christ in more of us" or put another way, "more of us in Christ". For this we need teaching. We also need admonishing, challenging, correcting. "Him we preach, warning every man and teaching every man in all wisdom, that we may present every man perfect in Christ Jesus. To this end I also labour, striving according to His working which works in me mightily," Col 1:28-29.

GLORIOUS VICTORY

The way St Paul describes his Christian ministry is no different to the process we each follow as we strive towards Christian maturity. We labour, struggling with all His energy, which so powerfully works in us. We work, and at the same time God works within us. A balance of cooperation between us and God. "Continue to work out your salvation with fear and trembling, for it is God who works in you to will and to act according to his good purpose," Php2:12-13. We work out our salvation as God works within us. Christ in you.

"Do your best, God does the rest." Christian maturity is something God develops within us. But we have to play our part so that the life of Christ is expressed in us. And what a wonderful goal that is to aim at. St Paul explains, "that their hearts may be encouraged, being knit together in love, and attaining to all riches of the full assurance of understanding, to the knowledge of the mystery of God, both of the Father and of Christ, in whom are hidden all the treasures of wisdom and knowledge," Col 2:2-3. This is what God promises us as we grow in Christian maturity: The full riches of complete understanding; knowing the mystery of God, namely Christ; all the treasures of wisdom and knowledge. In Eph3:8, St Paul uses a wonderful phrase to sum up all the blessings God has for us in His cosmic masterplan: "the unsearchable riches of Christ". God has so much to give us as we become mature in Christ!

Victorious New Testament believers are not living for the Lord, but it is actually the risen Christ living through them. St Paul's "old man" was dead through Christ (Rom6:2-11). He was truly free to live, but it wasn't actually St Paul who was living – it was Christ living through him. St Paul had learned the secret of victorious Christian living; it is not us living for Jesus, but Jesus living through us.

The Christian life is not just hard to live – it's impossible to live in our human strength. In the world, we live in Satan's territory. The only way to walk in victory is to let Christ live through us. St John encourages us saying, "You are of God, little children, and have overcome them, because He who is in you is greater than he who is in the world," 1Jn4:4. Jesus comforts us, "In the world you will have tribulation; but be of good cheer, I have overcome the world," Jn16:33. Jesus died on the cross for our sins, and then He was raised from the dead to rescue us and redeem us and reconcile us to God. But Christ then goes on working in our lives. And He doesn't just work from the outside but from the inside. Jesus is not on the outside of our lives, like a sculptor chipping away at our sinful thoughts and our bad habits. Christ is in us!

God is on the inside of our lives, living and working within us, filling our lives with the resurrection life of Christ Himself and transforming us into the image of Christ from inside us! "Christ in you – the hope of glory!!"

The road to heaven will not always be easy. But as he told the Roman Christians, and as St Paul himself experienced, the pathway to glory often includes suffering. The sufferings or tribulations we face are the pressures of a godless hostile world on those who follow Christ. "I now rejoice in my sufferings for you, and fill up in my flesh what is lacking in the afflictions of Christ, for the sake of

His body, which is the Church," Col 1:24.

"And not only that, but we also glory in tribulations, knowing that tribulation produces perseverance; and perseverance, character; and character, hope. Now hope does not disappoint, because the love of God has been poured out in our hearts by the Holy Spirit who was given to us," Rom5:3-5.

"Tribulations" is a strong term. It does not refer to minor inconveniences, but to real hardships. St Paul lived a life full of tribulation. St Paul knew the truth of this better than anyone. The bad we endure is not purposeless. God's plan is being carried out, and our troubles will make us the kind of people God can use. Even when things look bad, no one or no event can take away the promise of peace, hope, and joy. That can make any season a joyful one.

And instead of undermining our confidence in God, in fact these experiences of adversity and opposition strengthen our faith and build up our hope. Our hope comes through the resurrection life of Christ in us. Jesus has died – but He has also risen! And He has shown us the path we must follow, through suffering to glory, through the cross to resurrection. And in the end, all our suffering will be worth it.

Tribulation works or produces patience: the effect of afflictions on the minds of Christians is to make them patient. Sinners are irritated and troubled by them; they complain, and become more and more obstinate and rebellious. They have no sources of consolation; they deem God a hard master; and they become fretful and rebellious just in proportion to the depth and continuance of their trials. But in the mind of a Christian, who regards his Father's hand in it; who sees that he deserves no mercy; who has confidence in the wisdom and goodness of God; who feels that it is necessary for his own good to be afflicted; and who experiences its happy, subduing, and mild effect in restraining his sinful passions, and in weaning him from the world, the effect is to produce patience.

Accordingly, it will usually be found that those Christians who are longest and most severely afflicted are the most patient. Year after year of suffering produces increased peace and calmness of soul; and at the end of his course the Christian is more willing to be afflicted, and bears his afflictions more calmly, than at the beginning. He who on earth was most afflicted was the most patient of all sufferers; and not less patient when He was "led as a lamb to the slaughter", than when He experienced the first trial in His great work.

Endurance under trials, without sustaining loss or deterioration is a metaphor taken from refining metals, for example gold. St Peter writes in this regard, "In this you greatly rejoice, though now for a little while, if need be, you have been grieved by various trials, that the genuineness of your faith, being much more precious than gold that perishes, though it is tested by fire, may be found to praise, honour and glory at the revelation of Jesus Christ," 1Pt1:6-7.

We are not only happy for being in the state of communion with our God, and the prospect of being eternally with Him; but we glory in tribulations also. The promise of glory is also for the present time. No storm of circumstances can move us from where we stand. The fact that we are tightly, permanently moored to the dock of God's Grace provides (or should provide) us with a strong sense of security. Nothing can tear us away from God's Grace. We cannot be severed from God's loving acceptance of us in Christ (Eph1:6). Even our sin cannot separate us from our position of standing firm in God's Grace, for we are justified once and for all time. We continue to be in Christ by repentance. Christ is in you – the hope of glory!

All the sufferings we endure for the testimony of our Lord are so sanctified to us by His Grace, that they become powerful instruments of increasing our happiness. These are amazing words. St Paul does not write that "we endure tribulations", but that "we glory in tribulations". How can this be? It is because the tribulation is producing "patience" (perseverance), "experience" (proven character), and "hope". He alludes to the same idea in 2Co4:17, "For our light affliction, which is but for a moment, works for us a far more exceeding and eternal weight of glory."

Again, St Paul declared in Romans, "Yet in all these things we are more than conquerors through Him who loved us," Rom8:37. St Paul knows that we struggle in this life, and that we are afflicted with temptation and manifold weaknesses. He knows we mourn over continual sin, and the fear which such sinning brings, which is that we will fail and fall at last. So St Paul wants us to realise that in spite of all this, because God has purposed it, we will persevere to the end, and this is because God has done and is doing everything to make this glorious blessing a reality. Christ is in you!

St Paul says "I consider that our present sufferings are not worth comparing with the glory that will be revealed in us," Rom8:18. This necessity of conformity to Christ in suffering in order to participate in His glory, is taught alike by Christ Himself and by His apostles (Jn12:24-26; Mt16:24-25; 2Ti2:12). The sufferings of this life are not worth comparing with the glory which is to be revealed in us! The best is yet to come! "Earth has no sorrow which heaven cannot heal." Be reassured, however tough life gets, God will not let go of us. We will share in His glory! But how can we be certain? It's simple, says St Paul. Christ is in you – that's the hope of glory!

OUR HOPE OF GLORY

Christ is in you – the hope of glory! As Christians, we have God's glory in us, though God's glory is not fully revealed (Col 3:3-4). This is a very important statement. St Paul did not say that this glory would be revealed "to us" but rather "in us". The complete glory of God that most dream of receiving in eternity is already in us here on this earth! St Paul said, "He called you by our Gospel, to the obtaining of the glory of our Lord Jesus Christ," 2Th2:14. St Peter said he was a partaker of this "glory that shall be revealed," 1Pt5:1. St Paul also prayed for the Ephesians that the Lord would grant them the spirit of wisdom and revelation in the knowledge of Him so that they would see the glory of His inheritance that was already in the saints (Eph1:17-18).

The greatest miracle is Christ in you, the hope of glory. The grandest mystery of all St Paul tells us is Christ in you, the hope of glory. Christ in me creates the hope of glory. And what do you mean by the phrase, "the hope of glory", I mean that all the glory that could ever be will only be yours when Christ is in you. The only hope a man ever has for glory now, future, any time, under any condition is when Christ dwells within him, God wants to live in you, that's the message.

We may not reach Christian maturity in this life. None of us become perfect this side of heaven. But what St Paul is saying here is that Christ is in us now – and this is our guarantee that one day we will share in the glory of God. "Christ is in you, bringing with Him the hope of all the glorious things to come." We sometimes devalue the word "hope". In English, we can use "hope" to refer to some vague optimistic wish. In the Bible, the word "hope" is much more definite. When St Paul talks of "the hope of glory" he is actually saying "the happy certainty" of sharing God's glory.

Now hope is a combination of expectation and desire. I would love one day to walk on the moon. But since I have no expectation of that ever happening I can't say "I hope to walk on the moon." On the other hand, one day I am sure I will have to visit the dentist. But since I have no desire ever to visit the dentist again it would be wrong to say, "I hope to visit the dentist."

But my greatest desire is to spend eternity with Christ. And the promises of God make it absolutely certain that I will spend eternity with Christ. So, it is correct to say, I hope to spend eternity with Christ. I hope to share in His glory. This is not wishful thinking. This is expectation plus desire. This is the happy certainty of our Christian hope.

"And we rejoice in the hope of the glory of God. Not only so, but we also rejoice in our sufferings, because we know that suffering produces perseverance; perseverance, character; and character, hope. And hope does not disappoint us, because God has poured out his love into our hearts by the Holy Spirit, whom He has given us," Rom5:2-5.

We rejoice in the hope of sharing the glory of God. It has been said that man can live for 40 days without food, for three days without water, for several minutes without air but for only a few seconds without hope. Dostoevsky said, "Hell is hopelessness." The inscription above the entrance to Dante's inferno read, "Abandon hope all you who enter here."

True believers have every reason to be filled with hope. We have a hope which is steadfast and certain! "We rejoice in the hope of the glory of God." "Christ in you - the hope of glory!" Not some wishy washy optimism but a confident expectation. The happy certainty that one day, God will take us to be with Him and we will share His glory for eternity. This is our destiny as Christians. This is God's wonderful plan and purpose for us – yes even for you and even for me!

The indwelling Christ is the ground for the expectation of glory both now and the future. We received Christ's exalted resurrection life in Baptism and need to keep on seeking the ultimate and spiritual glories of the age to come. Christ in you, the hope of glory. The word glory points to the great consummation in God's eternal purpose, and is a comprehensive word for God's glorious presence with His people. Our ground of hope is Christ in you.

The full glory of the inheritance was a hope, to be realized when Christ should appear. Glory refers to the glory of the mystery; hence the glory consummated at Christ's coming is the glory which shall be revealed.

The glorified saints around the throne of God have no higher source of joy than the saints on earth. They have no higher theme or song of praise to the Father. They are only happier because their discovery of these things is more complete and are now freed from all earthly hindrances and limitations that interrupt our enjoyment in our present state.

Christ alone is our foundation for the blessed hope in the future, or eschatological glory. The fact that we now have Christ in us is the pledge of final glory when Christ returns. This glory is yet future. We will share in the yet future full manifestation of God's glory in Christ. St Paul wrote in Col 3:4, When Christ, who is our life, shall appear, then shall you also appear with Him in glory.

Jesus Christ focuses our minds and desires on that which is above in heaven and the eternal future. Christ in you gets eternity into the picture. He gets our minds off our past through the forgiveness of our sins and into the present as He lives within us and into the future as we concentrate on our blessed hope in Him alone. Christ in you energizes the present and gives us a song to sing. Lord Jesus, will I see You today? Even so, come!

If you know Jesus Christ as your personal Saviour He wants to settled down and make Himself permanently at home in your heart. He wants to settle down in your inner man that is, the personal, rational self, the moral I that has experienced spiritual renewal by the Spirit of God. He is talking about the very core of your inner spiritual being, the place where the Holy Spirit works to fashion and form His temple since the moment you were born again. That is the place where He is at work forming you in the image of Christ.

It is there St Paul tells us Christ dwells in your hearts through faith. Christ wants to settle down in a dwelling, to dwell fixedly in a place, to live in a home. He wants to settle down and feel completely at home as a permanent dwelling place in your heart.

 Do you make Christ feel at home? Do you invite Him in as a permanent resident? Does He feel comfortable in your heart? Are there two masters trying to be sovereign in your life? Do you give Christ the free reign of your life? Do you have any junk closets where He is forbidden to enter? Are there any secret hideouts in your heart? Can you honestly drag everything in your heart out in the glaring holy light of the Son?

The Christian has experienced the superior light and knowledge of Jesus Christ and all other religious experiences and claims of the Gnostics and secret mystery religions fade into nothing when compared to the inward knowledge of an intimate love relationship with Him.

The first Adam headed up the human race and stood for us, and fell for us, and we fell in him. How marvellous that the second Adam took up within Himself all His people and stood for us and kept the covenant with God the Father so that now every blessing of that new covenant is infallibly secure to all who are risen in Him.

THE RICHES OF THE GLORY OF THIS MYSTERY

When God's secrets break open, they do so in glory. The wealth of the root hidden in the ground is revealed in the hues of orchid or scent of rose. The hidden beauty of a beam of light is unravelled in the sevenfold colour of the rainbow. The swarming, infinitesimal life of southern seas breaks into waves of phosphorescence when cleft by the keel of the ship. And whenever the unseen world has revealed itself to mortal eyes, it has been in glory.

It was especially so at the Transfiguration, when the Lord's nature broke from the strong restraint within which He confined it and revealed itself to the eye of man. "And He was transfigured before them. His face shone like the sun, and His clothes became as white as the light," Mt17:2.

So when we accept the fact of His existence within us deeper than our own, and make it one of the aims of our life to draw on it and develop it, we shall be conscious of a glory transfiguring our life and irradiating ordinary things, such as will make earth, with its commonest engagements, like the vestibule of Heaven.

When this mystery or secret of the Divine life in man is apprehended and made use of, it gives great wealth to life. If all the treasures of wisdom, knowledge, power, and grace reside in Jesus, and He is become the cherished and honoured resident of our nature, it will be clear that we also must be greatly enriched. It is like a poor man having a millionaire friend come to live with him.

There are riches of patience. Life is not easy to any of us. No branch escapes the pruning knife; no jewel the wheel; no child the rod. People tyrannize over and vex us almost beyond endurance. Circumstances strain us till the chords of our hearts threaten to snap. Our nervous system is overtaxed by the rush and competition of our times. Indeed, we have need of patience!

Never to relax the self-watch; never to indulge in unkind or thoughtless criticism of others; never to utter the hasty word, or permit the sharp retort; never to complain except to God; never to permit hard and distrustful thoughts to lodge within the

soul; to be always more thoughtful of others than self; to detect the one blue spot in the clouded sky; to be on the alert to find an excuse for those who are forward and awkward, to suffer the aches and pains, the privations and trials of life, sweetly, submissively, trustfully; to drink the bitter cup, with the eye fixed on the Father's face, without a murmur or complaint: this needs patience, which mere stoicism could never give. And we cannot live such a life till we have learned to avail ourselves of the riches of the indwelling Christ.

When we dare to reckon on the indwelling of our glorious Lord, as King, Lawgiver, and Saviour, we can just start to realize the richness of this glory. He makes all grace to abound toward us, so that we have a sufficiency for all emergencies, and can abound in every good work. In His strength, ever rising up within us, we are able to do as much as those who are showered with the greatest mental and natural gifts, and we escape the temptations to vainglory and pride by which they are beset.

The Grace of purity and self-control, of fervent prayer and understanding in the Scriptures, of love for men and zeal for God, of lowliness and meekness, of gentleness and goodness - all is in Christ; and if Christ is in us, all is ours also. O that we would dare to believe it, and draw on it, letting down the pitcher of faith into the deep well of Christ's indwelling, opened within us by the Holy Spirit! (Jn7:38)

If only we would meet every call, difficulty, and trial, not saying, as we so often do, "I shall never be able to go through it", but saying, "I cannot; but Christ is in me, and He can", we should find that all trials were intended to reveal and unfold the wealth hidden within us, until Christ was literally formed within us, and His life manifested in our mortal body (2Co4:10).

Be still each day for a short time, sitting before God in meditation, and ask the Holy Spirit to reveal to you the truth of Christ's indwelling. Ask God to be pleased to make known to you what is the riches of the glory of this mystery (Col 1: 27).

Reverence your nature as the temple of the indwelling Lord. Be very careful of all that

> would defile the body or soil the soul. No beasts must herd in the temple courts. Get Christ to drive them out. Don't you know that you are a temple of God? The temple of God is holy, and so are you!

The amazing thing is the best is yet to come! These are words of hope and confident assurance of the believer's future. The apostle John wrote of that final glory in 1Jn3:1-3. What glory is ours, glory unspeakable! We shall have glorified bodies just like the resurrected body of Christ when He appears in glory. He who has come to live in our hearts, and reigns as our bosom's Lord, makes us glorious by His coming. When Christ comes to reign He brings countless blessings with Him.

Just think of it. He who went to the Cross for me will never be ashamed of me: He who gave me Himself will give me all heaven and more: He that opened His very heart to find blood and water to wash me in, how shall He keep back even His kingdom from me? O sweet Lord Jesus, You are indeed to us the hope, pledge, the guarantee of glory!

The Lord Jesus Christ entered into a covenant with God the Father to bring His people home to glory. He who pledged to bring every sheep of His flock safe to His Father's right hand will not fail. He has never failed one of His covenant promises. He never will.

Christ in you is glory. In having Christ, you have glory. As sure as the Lord God lives, Christ in you means you in glory with Him for all eternity. This is the most astounding truth taught in the Bible. Christ in you. Such glory, the certain pledge of the glory to be revealed, is within reach of each reader of these lines who will dare day by day to reckon that Christ lives within, and will be content to die to the energies and promptings for the self-life so that there may be room for the Christ-life to reveal itself. "I have been crucified with Christ; it is no longer I who live, but Christ lives in me; and the life which I now live in the flesh I live by faith in the Son of God, who loved me and gave Himself for me," Gal 2:20.

God was pleased to make known through St Paul "the riches of the glory of this mystery among the Gentiles; which is Christ in You, the hope of glory" (Col 1:27). This mystery is that the Lord Jesus is willing to dwell within the Gentile heart. That He should dwell in the heart of a child of Abraham was deemed a marvellous act of condescension; but that He should find a home in the heart of a Gentile was incredible.

The wealth of glory for the believer is this mystery among the Gentiles which is Christ. The mystery long hidden is not a diffusion of Christ among the Gentiles. It is the indwelling of Christ in His people, both Jewish and Gentile. It was not a mystery to the Jewish people that the Messiah should come and dwell among His people. That was their great hope. However, that the Messiah of Israel should dwell among the non-Jews was an entirely new revelation of the purposes of God. This is the greatest mystery of the universe that God of the Jewish people would take up residence in Gentile men and women. The idea of salvation of the Gentiles was nothing new. The prophets spoke of it and the poets wrote of it in the Psalms. But the idea that He would tabernacle Himself in a Gentile was something wholly new. Christ freely given to the Gentiles is the mystery; that is the mystery of Christ in you the hope of glory.

Christ now dwells in His people, regardless of whether they are Jewish or non-Jewish. It is Christ in you that gives us the riches of His glory. The declared hope of glory of both is Christ in you. St Paul has in mind the indwelling Christ in the heart of every believer. God desires for His

New Testament saints to know what the Old Testament saints could not know: "Christ in you, the hope of glory". The coming of the Messiah was predicted in the Old Testament, but the idea that He would actually indwell us was beyond anyone's imagination. Christ in me is a king demanding my loyalty as I bow in worship only to Him as my Lord and Master and as His servant I go out to serve. Don't be ashamed for one moment of the fact that Christ in you is your hope of glory.

Christ in me! That is my hope of glory and I pray that it is yours, too. It is the only hope for the world in which we live. Do you have that hope? Do you share that same expectation of glory with God in Christ? Do you have Christ dwelling within your heart? Do you have Christ in you? You can begin right now.

THE MYSTERY OF THE CHURCH

"By revelation He made known to me the mystery (as I have briefly written already, by which, when you read, you may understand my knowledge in the mystery of Christ), which in other ages was not made known to the sons of men, as it has now been revealed by the Spirit to His holy apostles and prophets: that the Gentiles should be fellow heirs, of the same body, and partakers of His promise in Christ through the Gospel," Eph3:3-6.

Our deepest passion must focus upon things too wonderful to be fully understood, such as "the Mystery of Christ". The Spirit has revealed through His holy apostles and prophets this mystery of Grace (Eph3:2-6). This mystery, which is God's master plan of salvation, was revealed in Our Lord Jesus Christ "for obedience to the faith" (Rom1:5). Mystery requires obedience without full knowledge. We are simply to trust and obey the plain truths of the Scriptures and grow in the knowledge of the Word every day! We must know enough not to deny what we cannot understand.

The divine mystery in Christ has revealed that believing

Gentiles are on the very same footing as Jewish believers. Gentiles are co-heirs with believing Jews (Eph3:6a). Since salvation involves the renewal of all mankind in Christ, the old distinction between Jew and Gentile no longer exists.

"Therefore, remember that you, once Gentiles in the flesh — who are called Uncircumcision by what is called the Circumcision made in the flesh by hands — that at that time you were without Christ, being aliens from the commonwealth of Israel and strangers from the covenants of promise, having no hope and without God in the world. But now in Christ Jesus you who once were far off have been brought near by the blood of Christ," Eph2:11-13.

This ethnic distinction was based on the flesh (Eph2:11), the Gentiles being uncircumcised and the Jews being circumcised. While Israel was especially blessed by God (Eph2:12), both Jews and Gentiles had to become true Israel (Eph2:13-18).

 "But now in Christ Jesus you who once were far off have been brought near by the blood of Christ. For He Himself is our peace, who has made both one, and has broken down the middle wall of separation, having abolished in His flesh the enmity, that is, the law of commandments contained in ordinances, so as to create in Himself one new man from the two, thus making peace, and that He might reconcile them both to God in one body through the cross, thereby putting to death the enmity. And He came and preached peace to you who were afar off and to those who were near. For through Him we both have access by one Spirit to the Father," Eph2:13-18.

Man's brokenness was twofold: man was separated from man, that is, the Gentile from the Jew (Eph2:13-15); and man was separated from God (Eph2:16-18). The healing is likewise twofold: the creation of a unified humanity, the Church, and the raising of this unified humanity to God. The Incarnation of the Son accomplished the former; His death and resurrection did the latter. The

whole Trinity, Father, Son and the Holy Spirit act together (Eph2:18).

"The middle-wall of separation" (Eph2:14) probably refers to the barrier in the temple separating the Court of the Gentiles from the Court of the Jews. This barrier manifested the limitations of the old covenant. It did not heal humanity's self-alienation; it actually increased human hostility. Now that this wall is "broken down", both Jews and Gentiles are reconciled and one in Christ.

The Church, humanity unified and renewed through union with the Incarnate Son of God (Eph2:11-18) is built on a foundation of "Jesus Christ and the apostles and prophets" (Eph2:20). Form this foundation come the Scriptures and all doctrine. In Eph4:11, these gifts are implied to be a continuing reality in the Church. The spiritual building is one: The Church is designed to be united.

The Church is important because it reveals Christ, even as Christ reveals God in human flesh. That is essentially what the Apostle St Paul is saying in 1Ti3:14-16. The Church is the continuing incarnation of God Incarnate. The word "incarnate" comes from two Latin words meaning "in flesh". It means that God took on a human body in the person of Jesus Christ. And since Jesus ascended into heaven, we now, as His body continue His presence on earth until He returns. Since the eternal destiny of every person on earth depends on his or her being rightly related to Jesus the coming King and Judge of all the earth, nothing could be more crucial than the Church!

So, in 1Ti3:15 St Paul is saying "the Church" is what holds up and holds firm the truth in the world. Again, this interpretation fits with St Paul's warnings not to be swayed by carnal philosophies (Col 2:8), false teachers (2Ti4:3), or any person who changes the Gospel (Gal 1:8). Rather than fall prey to false doctrine, we're to compare teachers to the Word of God (Acts17:11; 1Co4:6; 2Ti3:16; Rom15:4).

"And He Himself gave some to be apostles, some prophets, some evangelists, and some pastors and teachers, for the equipping of the saints for the work of ministry, for the edifying of the body of Christ, till we all come to the unity of the faith and of the knowledge of the Son of God, to a perfect man, to the measure of the stature of the fullness of Christ," Eph4:11-13.

The gifts listed in Eph4:11 are limited to those who lead the Church. The Holy Spirit extends gifts to each person at Chrismation, but the "ministry gifts" listed here form one leadership group responsible for "equipping" the laity for "the work of ministry" (Eph4:12).

GENTILES AND JEWS UNITED THROUGH THE GOSPEL

St Paul declares to the Romans, "For I am not ashamed of the Gospel of Christ, for it is the power of God to salvation for everyone who believes, for the Jew first and also for the Greek," Rom1:16. The power of God is seen in making men ministers of it, in the doctrines held forth in it, in the manner in which it was spread in the world, in the opposition it met with, in the continuance and increase of it notwithstanding the power and cunning of men, and in the shortness of time, in which so much good was done by it in the several parts of the world. It is the power of God organically or instrumentally, as it is a means made use of by God in quickening dead sinners, enlightening blind eyes, unstopping deaf ears, softening hard hearts, and making friends of enemies. To all this add the manner in which all this is done, suddenly, secretly, effectually, and by love, and not force.

The extent of this power is "to salvation". The Gospel is a declaration and revelation of salvation by Christ, and is a means of directing and encouraging souls to lay hold upon it and to everyone that believes. How does the Gospel become the power of God for salvation? It brings salvation only to those who believe. The Gospel was preached to the Jew first by Christ and His disciples; and even when it was ordered to be carried into the Gentile world, it was to begin with them, and became effectual for the salvation of many of them. After the Jews had rejected it, at that time, it was preached to the Gentiles with great success; which was the mystery hid from ages and generations past, but now made manifest.

In Rom1:16-17, the apostle brings forward a charge of sinfulness against all flesh, and declares the only method of deliverance from condemnation is by faith in the mercy of God, through Our Lord Jesus Christ. In Rom1:16, St Paul spoke of salvation - but what are we saved from? First and foremost, we are saved from the wrath of God that we righteously deserve. Unless there is something to be saved from, there is no point in talking about salvation. St Paul stressed that the righteousness of God will be expressed as wrath against all whose sins are unforgiven.

The Gentiles all sinned in the breaking of their law. The Jews all sinned in the breaking of their Law.

In addition, all people had been given the opportunity of coming to the knowledge of their sin and realizing their need for salvation from sin's consequences. The Jews thought themselves a holy people, entitled to their privileges by right, while they were unthankful, rebellious, and unrighteous. In Rom3:23 St Paul summed up the situation discussed in Rom1:18-3:20, "For all have sinned and fall short of the glory of God." St Paul says that all have sinned; no one deserves glory, honour and eternal life. The Jews could not be justified by the Law of Moses, any more than the Gentiles by the law of nature.

In Romans 2, St Paul explains that both Jews and Gentiles need the Gospel — everyone needs salvation, or rescue from judgment. "For as many as have sinned without Law will also perish without Law, and as many as have sinned in the Law will be judged by the Law," Rom2:12. Although some Jews claimed to have an advantage in salvation, St Paul explains that Jews are not immune to Sin and Judgment. St Paul says that that the Jews have a much greater need for Grace than the Gentiles. No matter who you are, if you sin, you will be condemned. Everyone is saved in the same way. So how do people become right with God?

"For when we were still without strength, in due time Christ died for the ungodly. For scarcely for a righteous man will one die; yet perhaps for a good man someone would even dare to die. But God demonstrates His own love toward us, in that while we were still sinners, Christ died for us," Rom5:6-8.

The human race is described as a sick man, whose disease is so far advanced that he is altogether without strength: no power remains in his system to throw off his mortal malady, nor does he desire to do so; he could not save himself from his disease if he would, and would not if he could. Man is still without strength; utterly helpless with no way of escape; still ailing; still sick (sin sick); unable to help ourselves; still powerless and too weak to help ourselves, totally unable to rescue ourselves from the effects of the Fall. Helpless in this context emphasizes moral frailty rather than physical weakness. We were quite powerless to help ourselves or even to understand.

When we were powerless to escape from our sin, powerless to escape death, powerless to resist Satan, and powerless to please Him in any way, God amazingly sent His Son to die on our behalf. Christ died for the ungodly and loved the unlovely. He loved us though there was nothing loveable in us. This is 'agape love'. It is selfless, sacrificial, unconditional love, the highest of the four types of love in the Bible. Our Lord Jesus lived out agape by sacrificing Himself for the sins of the world.

The Spirit of God wants to convey to us the truth, which we are always slow to receive, that Christ did not die because men were good, or would be good, but died for them as ungodly. In other words, "He came to seek and to save that which was lost," Lk19:10. St Paul mentioned the idea of a substitutionary sacrifice with the word propitiation in Rom3:25. Here, he makes the point again by saying that Christ died for the ungodly. Who are the ungodly and wicked people Our Lord Jesus died for? St Paul spent the first two-and-a-half chapters of the Book of Romans telling us that we all are those people. If Christ died for the ungodly, this fact leaves the ungodly no excuse if they do not come to Him, and believe in Him unto salvation. Had it been otherwise they might have pleaded,

'We are not fit to come.' But you are ungodly, and Christ died for the ungodly, why not for you?

Therefore, to genuinely say, "Our Lord Jesus died for me" you must also say, "I have no strength to save myself. I am ungodly. I am a sinner." Our Lord Jesus died to save and transform these. You will say: "Oh, I am one of the worst in the world." Christ died for the worst in the world. "Oh, but I have no power to be better." Christ died for those that were without strength. "Oh, but my case condemns itself." Christ died for those that legally are condemned. "OK, but my case is hopeless." Christ died for the hopeless. He is the hope of the hopeless. He is the Saviour not of those partly lost, but of the wholly lost.

It's hard to love the weak and powerless, but when those same people are also ungodly (opposed to all that God stands for) that kind of love is amazing. The love of God is without any cause outside of Himself. Christ died for us while we were unable to obey Him, and without ability to save ourselves. This weakness or inability is no doubt sinful; but it is our inability, not our guilt, that the Apostle here designates. When we were unable to keep the Law of God, or do anything towards our deliverance from Divine wrath, Christ interposed, and died for those whom He came to redeem. And it was when we were yet plunged in this repulsive state of impotence (helplessness) and ungodliness that the greatest proof of love was given us, in that Christ died for us. God loves us just the way we are, but He loves us too much to leave us the way we are (Jn15:16, Php1:6)! St Paul describes the greatness of God's love. It is love given to the undeserving, to those without strength, to the ungodly, to sinners. This emphasizes the fact that the reasons for God's love are found in Him, not in us.

 We all know that human love is almost invariably based on the attractiveness of the object of love, and thus men and women are inclined to love those who reciprocate love to us. This same quality of love is therefore falsely ascribed to God. How many (even believers) think that God's love for us is dependent on how good we are or how much we serve Him, etc.! But as Our Lord Jesus

> taught, even the tax collectors loved those who loved them (Mt5:46).

Looking back, we see the great love of God to us in the gift of His dear Son for us when there was nothing good in us, and when we were ungodly, when we had no power to produce anything good, for we were without strength, at such a time. Even at such a time, Christ came on wings of love, and up to the bloody tree He went, and laid down His life for our deliverance. We, therefore, feel confident that He will not leave us now, and that He will not keep back anything from us whatever we may need. He has committed Himself to the work of our eternal salvation. He has done too much for us already ever to run back from His purpose; and in our worst estate, if we are in that condition now, we may still confidently appeal to Him, and rest quite sure that He will bring us up even to the heights of joy and safety.

St Chrysostom: There is no one who will save us except the One who loved us so much that while we were yet sinners, He died for us. Do you see what ground this gives for us to hope? For before this, there were

two difficulties in the way of our being saved. First we were sinners, and second, our salvation required the Lord's death, something which was quite incredible before it happened and which required enormous love for it to happen at all. But now that it happened, the rest becomes that much easier.

"But God demonstrates His own love, in that while we were still sinners, Christ died for us," Rom5:8. How does the death of the Son demonstrate the love of the Father? Because it was harder for the Father to send His Only Son, and because God (the Father) was in Christ, reconciling the world to Himself (2Co5:19). The work of Our Lord Jesus on the cross for us is God's ultimate proof of His love for us. He may give additional proof, but He can give no greater proof. If the Cross is the ultimate demonstration of God's love, it is also the ultimate demonstration of man's hatred. It also proves that the height of man's hatred can't defeat the height of God's love. Again, the demonstration of God's love isn't displayed so much in that Our Lord Jesus died, but it is seen in whom Our Lord Jesus died for - undeserving sinners and rebels against Him. And He loved us totally then! And He will love us to the end and forever!

This will take an eternity to comprehend!

VICTORY OVER DEATH

By dying on the cross and rising from the dead, Our Lord Jesus Christ cleansed the world from evil and sin. He defeated the devil "in his own territory" and on "His own terms". The "wages of sin is death," Rom6:23. So the Son of God became man and took upon Himself the sins of the world and died a voluntary death. By His sinless and innocent death accomplished entirely by His free will, and not by physical, moral, or juridical necessity, He made death to die and to become itself the source and the way into life eternal. This is what the Church sings on the feast of the Resurrection, the New Passover in Christ, the new Paschal Lamb, who is risen from the dead: Christ is risen from the dead! Trampling down death by death! And upon those in the tombs bestowing life!

But in fact, Christ has been raised from the dead, the firstfruits of those who have fallen asleep. For as by a man there came death, by a Man has come also the resurrection of the dead. "For as in Adam all die, so also in Christ shall all be made alive," 1Co15:22.

 St Cyril of Alexandria contemplated: "I am dying for all men", says the Lord. "I am dying to give them life through Myself and to redeem the whole human race through My humanity. In My death, death itself will die and man's fallen nature will rise again with Me. I wanted to be like My brothers in every respect, so I became a man like you, a descendant of Abraham." Understanding this well St Paul says: "As the children of a family share the same flesh and blood, He too shared our human nature so that by His death, He could destroy the power of the devil, the prince of death." Death itself and the prince of death could be destroyed only by Christ, who is above all, giving Himself up as a ransom for all.

The destruction of death by Christ's own death is the transformation of death itself into an act of life. It is the recreation of Sheol — the spiritual condition of being dead — into the paradise of God. Thus, in and through the death of Our Lord Jesus Christ, death is made "to die". In Him, who is the Resurrection and the Life, man cannot

die, but lives forever with God. "Truly, truly I say to you, he who hears my word and believes in Him who sent Me has eternal life; he does not come into judgment, but has passed from death into life," Jn5:24.

"And not only that, but we also rejoice in God through our Lord Jesus Christ, through whom we have now received the reconciliation," Rom5:11. But we also rejoice in God through Our Lord Jesus Christ, through whom we have now received the reconciliation: With the Incarnation, God has assumed and glorified our flesh and has consecrated and sanctified our humanity (Jn17:19). Through His Incarnation He is joined to our humanity and glorifies it in Himself, uniting us to God, fulfilling the purpose of our creation in Genesis. We are created in God's image. Through sin, that image has been greatly broken and damaged, but through redemption in Christ it is renewed "according to the image of Him who created it" (Col 3:10). Christ's crucifixion delivered our fallen humanity from sin and death and raised us up with Him in His resurrection. Christ has made atonements for us, and God has accepted that atonement on our behalf.

And the ground of this joy is the expiation of sin by Christ, by whom we have now received the atonement;

atonement is not made, but received by us; which denotes the application of the atoning blood and sacrifice of Christ to the conscience, the Spirit's witness of interest in it, and the office of faith, as a recipient of it: faith receives it from Him, and by Him; which, as it is the ground of present rejoicing in God, so it is the foundation of hope of future glory.

The word "now" refers to the Gospel dispensation. The poor Jews are at the utmost loss about atonement: sometimes they tell us it is by confession, repentance, and good works; sometimes by beneficence and hospitality; sometimes they say their captivity is their atonement; and, at other times, that death expiates all their sins. Blessed be God for the atoning sacrifice of Christ!

The righteousness God requires is available in Christ to anyone who will receive it by faith. This salvation by faith has always been the way God has made men righteous, so that He could save and bless them. It was so with Abraham, and everyone who, like Abraham, believes in God's promise of salvation. By faith, one becomes a son of Abraham. Circumcision and Law-keeping did not save Abraham; faith did. So it is for all men, throughout all times.

St Chrysostom: The fact that we who were such terrible sinners were saved is a very great sign, indicating how much we were loved by Him who saved us. For it was not by angels or archangels but by His Only Begotten Son that God save us!

GENTILES AS WELL AS JEWS ARE FREE FROM THE LAW

The old covenant Law is no longer binding on believers in Christ (Eph2:14-15). "For sin shall not have dominion over you, for you are not under Law but under Grace," Rom6:14. If we were under the authority of the Law, then we would be condemned as sinners, and Sin would have the final say in our lives. We would die. But we are not under the Law, and not under its penalty. Death has been conquered, the power of Sin has been broken, and the captives of Sin have been set free!

Since we are under Grace, Sin is not our master. The important truth to retain is that God's all sufficient Grace enables each of His children to do what He calls us to do that we might be pleasing to Him. Grace (Rom6:15) is the resurrection power (transforming power, power to obey) available to every believer in Christ. Stated succinctly Grace is not a license to do as we please, but is the power to obey as we should. Grace is God's enabling me to "turn off" my flesh. Grace is God's Spirit enabling me to overcome Sin, moment by moment, day by day. I cannot overcome Sin...it will overcome me if I try in my power. All attempts to defeat the flesh in my own power will fail (Rom7:14-25).

"But now we have been delivered from the Law, having died to what we were held by, so that we should serve in the newness of the Spirit and not in the oldness of the letter," Rom7:6. This verse states the consequences of the Gospel, in distinction from the effects of the Law. Believers now have the power when led by the Holy Spirit to say "yes" to God and "no" to the flesh, whereas before our union with Christ took place (Rom6:1-11), we had no choice. St Paul teaches clearly that the flesh is opposed to Spirit. The unbeliever can live only in the flesh; the believer can live in the Spirit but can fall back into living according to the flesh. St Paul repeatedly encourages believers to overcome the deeds of the flesh in the only way possible - by living in the Spirit.

"For Christ is the end of the Law for righteousness to everyone that believes," Rom10:4. Some translations say the "goal" of the Law, or the purpose of the Law. Both goal and end can be supported by other verses, but which emphasis did St Paul intend here? In a race, for example, the goal is also the end. When we reach the goal or purpose of some endeavour, the project is finished. Christ is the supreme expression of the Law. Now that we have Him, we do not need the preliminary, for He is the means of our righteousness.

The endless debates centring on the word "end" are all futile in their efforts to abrogate the Law of God. It is contrary to Christ who came to establish the Law (Ps40:8; Mt5:17). The ultimate point or thing at which the Law directs its view, that is, the object intended to be reached or accomplished is righteousness. Christ is the only righteous One having faced the incessant temptations of the flesh and defeated them. Christ has always been the way of salvation in both testaments.

St Severian: This does not mean that Christ is part of the Law but rather that He is the beginning of a new life. The Law has come to an end; it has ceased.

The strictness of the Law showed men their need of salvation by Grace, through faith. And the ceremonies shadowed forth Christ as fulfilling the righteousness, and bearing the curse of the Law. So, that even under the Law, all who were justified before God, obtained that blessing by faith, whereby they were made partakers of the perfect righteousness of the promised Redeemer. The Law is not destroyed, nor the intention of the Lawgiver disappointed; but full satisfaction being made by the death of Christ for our breach of the Law, the end is gained. That is, Christ has fulfilled the whole Law, therefore whoever believes in Him, is counted just before God, as much as though he had fulfilled the whole Law Himself. Sinners never could go on in vain fancies of their own righteousness, if they knew the justice of God as a Governor, or His righteousness as a Saviour.

The vital knowledge necessary for being straightened out is by faith in Christ. "For Christ is the end of the Law for righteousness to everyone that believes," Rom10:4. St Paul's conclusion is clear enough: Righteousness cannot be obtained through our efforts to keep the Law. Rather, it must be:

- given through Christ,
- received by faith rather than works, and
- available to Gentiles as well as Jews.

When it comes to salvation, Jews do not have special privileges. The Law, which was given to Israel, is not the means of salvation. The old covenant included faith, but it emphasized obedience. Since no one could do everything the Law required, it could never be a means of righteousness. The Law will not falsify the facts. It is a perfect description of righteousness. The Law was given for life-giving purposes (Rom10:5). Man sinned and he could not keep the Law. Any theory of justifying man's sin by a book transaction that by-passes a change of heart and reconciliation to God and His Law, is a legal fiction and rightly termed an anti-Law Gospel. The new covenant, however, is based on Christ, so it succeeds where the old covenant could not.

EVERYONE IS INVITED

In fellowship with Christ the believer is never alone or exposed to embarrassment and shame. "For the scripture says," St Paul notes in verse 11, "Everyone who believes in Him will not be put to shame," Rom10:11 This is quoted from Is28:16, which says that God will lay a cornerstone in Zion for a sure foundation, and people who have faith in this cornerstone will not be found short on the Day of Judgment. St Paul quoted the entire verse in Rom9:33; here he just repeats the part about believing in Christ as the key to salvation.

St Paul then repeats a favourite theme: "For there is no distinction between the Jew and the Greek, for the same Lord is Lord of all, who richly blesses all who call on Him. For everyone who calls on the name of the Lord will be saved," Rom10:12-13, quoting Joel 2:32. Salvation comes by calling on the Lord, looking to Him for salvation. In Joel, the Lord was Yahweh, but St Paul uses the verse for Christ, showing that he accepted Jesus as God. God calls everyone by name to Himself. God has called everyone to salvation in Christ. Christ has opened up the heavenly storehouse and raided the divine treasury and we "sit together in heavenly places in Christ Jesus" (Eph2:6). The call of God to every sinner means that His word shall not return unto Him void. "For whosoever shall call upon the name of the Lord shall be saved," Rom10:13. There is an appropriate response of thankfulness that must resonate in the heart of the believer.

God does have methods of reaching hearts other than missions. However, God has always involved His Church of the Old Testament and the Church of the New Testament in a mission-based operation of proclaiming the good news of salvation to all mankind. "How then shall they call on Him in whom they have not believed? and how shall they believe in Him of whom they have not heard? and how shall they hear without a preacher?" Rom10:14.

Salvation comes by accepting Jesus Christ as Lord. The problem is that St Paul's own people are rejecting the message. He highlights this in verse 14: "How then shall they call on Him in whom they have not believed?" Rom10:14. They have to call on the Lord to be saved, but if people think He is a crucified criminal instead of the Messiah, they won't call on Him.

"And how shall they believe in Him of whom they have not heard? And how shall they hear without a preacher? And how shall they preach unless they are sent?" Rom10:14-15. Messengers were sent: "As it is written, 'how beautiful are the feet of them that preach the Gospel of peace, and bring glad tidings of good things!'," Rom10:15. This is quoted from the Greek version of Is52:7, which uses the common New Testament verb for preaching the Gospel.

In Isaiah's day, the good news was the prophecy of the people being restored to their land.

THE GENTILES' SALVATION

Regardless of one's background, repentance and faith are what qualifies one to enter the Kingdom of God. The unbelief of the Jews opened the door to salvation for the Gentiles. It would be a two-for-one success, if St Paul's Gentile mission could "provoke" the Jews to salvation. If they could witness the Grace of God working in the lives of Gentiles, it might grab their attention (Rom11:14). The shame and nakedness that comes from Old Covenant-inspired Jewish religion might be put in stark contrast with the sunlit New Covenant Grace and love that is saving the Gentiles. Who are the Gentiles? St Paul describes them in Eph2:1-12 as those who are Gentiles by birth, uncircumcised, separate from Christ, excluded from the citizenship of Israel, foreigners to the covenants of the promise, dead in trespasses and sins, ruled by Satan, slaves to sinful passions, objects of God's wrath, without hope and without God, children of disobedience.

But all of a sudden, the Gospel came to the Gentiles. The sun rose, the darkness was dispelled, and they were made alive in Christ. They were enabled to repent of their sins and trust in Jesus Christ. They were justified and adopted as sons of God. They were indwelt by the Holy Spirit and became people of the Holy Scriptures. Jesus said, "But many who are first will be last, and many who are last will be first," Mt19:30. Based on the terms of the New Covenant, the Gentiles had equal access to the Kingdom of Heaven, although they had not served God under the Old Covenant. The Jews, who had laboured long under the Old Covenant, were jealous of the Grace extended to the Gentile "newcomers". The Jews who were first in privilege, yet they are not first in the Kingdom. Jesus told the Pharisees that the sinners they despised were being saved ahead of them: "Truly I tell you, the tax collectors and the prostitutes are entering the Kingdom of God ahead of you," Mt21:31–32.

Thus, through the unbelief of Israel, God opened the door of the Gospel to the Gentiles. To a Gentile's question, "What must I do to be saved?" St Paul gave the answer: "Believe on the Lord Jesus Christ and you will be saved" (Acts16:30-31). Whether Jew or Gentile, we are saved by Grace alone through faith alone in Christ alone, plus nothing. The Jews refused to embrace their Saviour

Messiah. But God cannot be frustrated. He opened the door to the Gentiles, who gladly believed on the Lord Jesus and were saved. For we read, "That if you confess with your mouth, 'Jesus is Lord', and 'believe in your heart that God raised him from the dead', you will be saved," Rom10:9.

ONE AND SAME NEW COVENANT PROMISE IN CHRIST

Believing Jews and Gentiles do not exist in two different covenants, but share equally in the one and same new covenant promise in Christ (Eph3:6c). There is not one God to the Jews, more kind, and another to the Gentiles, who is less kind; the Lord is a Father to all men. The promise is the same to all, who call on the name of the Lord Jesus as the Son of God, as God manifest in the flesh.

All believers who thus call upon the Lord Jesus, and none else, will do so humbly or sincerely. But how should any call on the Lord Jesus, the Divine Saviour, who had not heard of Him? And what is the life of a Christian but a life of prayer? It shows that we feel our dependence on Him, and are ready to give up ourselves to Him, and have a believing expectation of our all from Him. It was necessary that the

Gospel should be preached to the Gentiles. Somebody must show them what they are to believe.

How does St Paul fit into the cosmic plan described in Eph1:3-14 and Eph2:1-22? God has revealed this plan to him (Eph3:1-6) so that he can reveal it to all, especially to the Gentiles (Eph3:7-13). The content of the revelation (Eph3:3) is that through the Gospel the Gentiles should be united with the Jews, so that a united and renewed humanity is brought to God. Why did God choose a Jew to preach to the Gentiles? This is because if God can redeem Saul, the persecutor of the Church and hater of Gentiles, then God can certainly redeem the Gentiles through Saul.

How welcome the Gospel ought to be to those to whom it was preached! The Gospel is given, not only to be known and believed, but to be obeyed. It is not a system of notions, but a rule of practice. The beginning, progress, and strength of faith is by hearing. But it is only hearing the Word, as the Word of God that will strengthen faith.

This truth, this unity of Gentiles and Jews in the Body

of Christ, had not been previously made known. St Paul said that this truth about Christ had been kept secret since the world began (Rom16:25, 26; 1Co2:7). Not only did men not know of God's mystery (Eph3:5), neither did the angels. They hear about it from men. How can this be? It is because "the Church" affects all elements of creation, from the material to the immaterial. The united renewed humanity made possible by Christ is the basis of reconciliation of the heavens and the earth. Therefore, the Church ascends the angels, "the principalities and the powers". The basis of such astounding work by men is Christ's resurrection and exultation (Eph3:11).

God kept this great secret, for had the princes of this world (including the Devil) known it they would not have crucified the Lord of glory. If Satan had known that anyone who believed would get born again of God's spirit, be justified (just as if they never sinned), be made righteous, and complete in Christ with eternal life, he never would have crucified Jesus Christ. He would rather have had Jesus walking the earth declaring God's Word than to have it available for every believer to be made perfect in Christ.

It was an "unsearchable" truth because it was "hid in God!" The things that God had planned for us, He kept secret from ages and generations and revealed them after all was accomplished and Holy Spirit given on the day of Pentecost. The greatness of this mystery is that each believer is perfect in Christ: completely, completely, absolutely complete in Christ. The riches of the glory of this mystery is that it is

THE MYSTERY OF ISRAEL'S TEMPORARY BLINDNESS

 St Paul then says: "For I do not desire, brethren, that you should be ignorant of this Mystery, lest you should be wise in your own opinion, that blindness in part has happened to Israel until the fullness of the Gentiles has come in," RomII:25.

It is the engrafting of the Gentiles which supplies the perfect "fullness" of the good olive tree (the Abrahamic tree). It restores its majestic appearance and fruitfulness.

St Paul seems to put aside his formal style of discourse or diatribe, and he is overtaken by a revelation from God for the Gentiles to whom he had been called. Now he seems to see all the Mystery of the Divine purpose unfolded before him, and he breaks away from the restrained and formal method of argument he has imposed upon himself. Just as when treating the glory of the Resurrection, his argument passes into revelation, 'Behold, I tell you a Mystery' (1Co15:51); so here he declares not merely as the result of his argument, but as an authoritative revelation, the mystery of the Divine purpose. St Paul calls it a Mystery, something previously hidden but now revealed — and it is revealed so Gentiles do not think themselves superior to Jews. It was God's plan for Israel to resist their own Messiah, for a while. Most of the Jews did not accept Jesus. But this resistance is temporary — it lasts only until the full number of Gentiles comes into faith.

St Paul shares this revelation for a specific purpose: so that Gentile believers will not be wise in their own estimation, or so that they will not be puffed up with pride over their position before God as contrasted with the present status of the nation of Israel. The mystery that St Paul reveals is: "That a hardness has happened in part to Israel until the fullness of the Gentiles comes in, and so all Israel will be saved." St Paul was confident that an understanding of this truth would keep the Gentile believers from the sin of boasting over Israel.

The context of this passage also confirms that the hardening referred to only part of the individuals who compose the nation of Israel. This truth was dealt with in Rom11:5, 7, 17. Only the remnant, the elect of Israel, is being saved now. Only some branches, not all, were broken off the good olive tree. This condition prevails in Israel today. The hardening process is affecting only part of the nation. The implication of Rom11:1-10 is that only some of the people were hardened as evidenced by the fact that individual Jews were indeed being justified by faith in their Messiah, such as the apostle St Paul who was "an Israelite, a descendant of Abraham, of the tribe of Benjamin" (Rom11:1).

St Theodoret of Cyr: St Paul insists that only part of Israel has been hardened, for in fact many of them believe. He thus encourages them not to despair that others will be saved as well. After the Gentiles accepted the Gospel, the Jews would believe, when the great Elijah would come to them and bring them the doctrine of faith. The Lord Himself said as much: "Elijah will come and restore all things," Mt17:11; Mk9:12.

"I say then, have they stumbled that they should fall? Certainly not! But through their fall, to provoke them to jealousy, salvation has come to the Gentiles. Now if their fall is riches for the world, and their failure riches for the Gentiles, how much more their fullness! For I speak to you Gentiles; inasmuch as I am an apostle to the Gentiles, I magnify my ministry, if by any means I may provoke to jealousy those who are my flesh and save some of them. For if their being cast away is the reconciling of the world, what will their acceptance be but life from the dead?" RomII:II-15.

The fall of the Jews, their blindness, their hardening, can be revoked; it is not necessarily inevitable that Israel should fall permanently. The only miracle now that could prevent the complete and utter collapse of the Jews' salvation is to see something that they have never seen before. What God believes will happen for the Jews is that they will see He loves them in such a selfless way as demonstrated at the Cross, just as He loves the Gentiles and gives them salvation through Jesus' sacrifice. Such divine love for the Gentiles will provoke the jealousy of His Israelites.

Jews who reject Christ are not hopelessly lost — they can still be saved. But in the meantime, salvation is being offered to Gentiles. St Paul is alluding here to Dt32:21: "I will make them jealous with a people they do not recognize, with a nation slow to learn I will enrage them." Contrary to what most Jews thought, God would bless the

Gentiles so much that the Jews would be envious. That is St Paul's hope and reason for ministry.

If the failure of the Jews brought salvation to everyone else, won't it be even better when the Jews finally accept the Gospel? They might be spiritually dead now, but God can raise the dead. What is the remedy for spiritual death? The answer is found in the illustration of the good olive tree. Christ is the olive tree. Everything — the olives, the knob, the branches — that is connected with Him, who is the Root, is holy.

St Paul envisions a regrafting of the dead branches when the Jews believe in the Root. "And they also, if they do not continue in unbelief, will be grafted in, for God is able to graft them in again," Rom11:23. Here is the resurrection from the dead! If the Jews accept the Messiah, they will be re-attached to the Abrahamic tree — everything can change, according to whether people accept or reject Christ. God does not favour one ethnic group over the other.

St Paul then reasons as to how easy it will be for the Jews to be brought back in: "For if you (Gentiles) were cut off from what is by nature a wild olive tree, and grafted, contrary to nature, into a cultivated olive tree..." — if that difficult thing has been done — "how much more will these natural branches (Jews) be grafted back into their own olive tree?" Rom11:24. God can easily put the Jews back in. The unnatural process of grafting from a wild to a good olive tree is a miracle of God's Grace to the Gentiles. Likewise, the regrafting process of the dead branches again to the good olive tree, is a miracle of God's Grace.

St Paul certainly incorporates hints of the future salvation of Israel: "What will their acceptance be but life from the dead?" Rom11:15. The problem with Jewish unbelief in Christ is that it results in separation from God and ultimately death. "And they also, if they do not continue in unbelief, will be grafted in, for God is able to graft them in again...How much more will these who are the natural branches be grafted into their own olive tree?" Rom11:24.

The good olive tree represents the Mystery of the Gospel (Col 1:26-27), "which is Christ in you" and "abide in Me and I in you" (Jn15:4). There is nothing more sad than a flourishing tree which has been blighted by disease and trimmed to a hideous shadow of its former greatness. The Gospel is the greatest riches of every place where it is. As therefore the righteous rejection of the unbelieving Jews, was the occasion of so large a multitude of the Gentiles being reconciled to God, and at peace with Him; the future receiving of the Jews into the Church would be such a change, as would resemble a general resurrection of the dead in sin to a life of righteousness.

"For I do not desire, brethren, that you should be ignorant of this Mystery, lest you should be wise in your own opinion, that blindness in part has happened to Israel until the fullness of the Gentiles has come in," Rom11:25. In verse 25 the apostle states that the hardening has come upon part of Israel. The divine hardening (in punishment for human hardening) affects part of the people in any period of history. With respect to Israel this partial hardening began already during the days of the old dispensation (Rom9:27; 10:16, 21; 11:13), was taking place in St Paul's own day, and will continue until the close of the new dispensation. It is obvious that if, in every age, some Israelites are hardened, it must also be true that in every age some are saved. However, Israel, as a nation, will not be saved until they go through 'the time of Jacob's trouble' (Jer30:7). St Paul's statement in Rom11:25 indicates that this partial hardening will prevail until 'they shall look unto Me whom they have pierced' (Zec12:10), and say, 'Blessed is He that comes in the name of the Lord' (Mt23:39; Ps118:26).

As was mentioned previously, Israel's national salvation will not occur "until the fullness of the Gentiles comes in" (Rom11:25), and it is important to establish the correct interpretation of the phrase "fullness of the Gentiles". Commentators are almost unanimous in their opinion that this phrase is a numerical reference. By "fullness" the apostle means full number. What St Paul is saying, then, here in verse 25 is that Israel's partial hardening - the hardening of part of the people of Israel - will last until the full number of elect Gentiles has been gathered into God's fold. The complete number should not be translated in such a way as to suggest 'all'. It is rather 'the number that should be', 'the determined number', or 'the number determined by God'. The fullness of the Gentiles is the number of Gentile believers, all the sheep 'not of this fold', which Jesus will also bring (Jn10:16). The fullness of the Gentiles, then, is related to the number of believers which God is calling from among the nations other than Israel.

The Greek word translated as fullness means 'a full number' or 'a complete number'. After the fullness of the

Gentiles has come in, after that number foreknown to God is reached, then all Israel will be saved. According to Acts15:14, one of the purposes of the Church Age is to call out from among the Gentiles a people for His name. This calling out from among the Gentiles will continue until the fullness, that set number of Gentiles, is reached. This interpretation does not deny the fact that God is still calling both Jews and Gentiles into the Church during this present dispensation, or that God also counts the elect Jews who are being saved. It actually implies that the full number of Jewish believers will have entered the Church by that point as well. This verse simply states that God uses the non-Jewish believers as a reference point and that when the full number of elect Gentiles has come in, He will resume His work with national Israel which will result in their "fullness" (Rom11:12).

"And so all Israel will be saved, as it is written: 'The Deliverer will come out of Zion, And He will turn away ungodliness from Jacob'; 'For this is My Covenant with them, When I take away their sins'," Rom11:26-27, quoting Is59:20-21; 27:9; and Jer31:33-34.

ISRAEL OF THE END TIME

Rom11:26a declares that at that time, "All Israel will be saved". The apostle declares a great and general conversion of the Jewish people, which should take place when the fullness of the Gentiles had been brought in, and that then, and not until then, those prophecies should be fully accomplished which speak of the salvation of Israel. He contemplated something more than merely the silent addition of a few Israelites to the Church during successive ages. It is evident that St Paul meant to say, that the Jews were to be restored in the same way in which they were then rejected. The nation of Israel as a whole, being composed of every Israelite without exception, has been set aside by God during the present dispensation. He is currently working only with the few members of the believing remnant of Israel who are entering the Church. This is the people which should have introduced all the other peoples into the "Kingdom"; and for their punishment the opposite is what will take place, as Jesus had declared: 'The first shall be last' (M20:16).

"All Israel", evidently signifies Israel taken in its entirety. Does this mean that every Israelite who has ever lived will ultimately be saved? At that future time,

God will again work with every individual member of the nation of Israel. But how is it possible for God to bring every living member of the nation to salvation in Christ without violating His established practice of receiving only the believing remnant, as was evident throughout Romans 9-11? Does not Rom9:27 plainly state that, "Only the remnant will be saved?" Since this is clearly the case, what can be inferred is that no unbelieving Israelite will survive the 'time of Jacob's trouble', the time of the Great Tribulation - that the entire nation of Israel at the Second Coming of Christ will be composed of believing Israelites who are looking for the soon return of their Messiah.

In this regard, all Israel of Rom11:26a is the real, elect, spared nation of the future - 'those written unto life' (Dan12:1; Is4:3). The Mystery comprehends this fact, for the salvation of national Israel was impossible except on purely Grace lines. God had given them the Law that was necessary to reveal sin. But they utterly failed. Now comes in the fullness of the Gentiles - by Grace; and so, after that, and on the same Grace line as were the Gentiles, all Israel shall be saved! Most of that earthly nation will perish under Divine judgments and the Antichrist; but the Remnant will be 'accounted as a generation'.

This is not a contradiction if it is understood in the context of Israel's national salvation. As Zec13:8-9 has pointed out, two-thirds of the Jewish population will be destroyed in the persecutions of the Tribulation. This will include the entire non-remnant so that only the remnant will survive: the escaped of Is4:2; 10:20; 37:31-32; Joel 2:32; and Obadiah 17. This is a plausible explanation for how the Lord can work only with the believing remnant and yet save every living individual from the nation of Israel in those last days.

St Paul has already argued that the Jews have not stumbled beyond recovery (Rom11:11-15), and Jewish branches can be grafted back in if they believe, so when he says they are hardened until the full number of Gentiles comes in, he implies that the hardening was temporary. He also says that the Jewish people are still loved, their calling cannot be revoked, and that God will have mercy on them. St Paul believes that most of the Jews will be saved, because Deuteronomy 32 predicts a time when they will accept Jesus as their Saviour.

Some scholars say that "all Israel" means all Jews. But there is no blanket promise that absolutely every Jewish person will be saved, or will come to faith. St Paul's anguish expressed in Rom9:1-3 would be unnecessary if they were all going to be saved anyway. Other scholars say that "all Israel" means "all God's people", as St Paul has redefined them: those who believe in Jesus are now the Israel of God, all who are attached to the Abrahamic tree through faith. St Paul believes that this will include "the full number of the Gentiles" as well as a sizeable number of Jews who are stirred up by seeing the blessings being given to Gentiles. There you have the whole story. The coming in of the fullness of the Gentiles, the filling up of the number of Israel, the conversion of both Jews and Gentiles.

When St Paul stated all Israel, he meant all Jews living at that time, not all Jews of all time. The Bible speaks of all Israel, the whole congregation of Israel, coming out of Egypt at the Exodus. Of course, not all Jews who ever lived came out of Egypt, but every Jew who lived at that time did come out of Egypt. This is the same way Rom11:26a should be interpreted. It means that every Jew living at the time will be saved.

The Gentile engraftment project is so that "all Israel shall be saved"; "And so all Israel shall be saved: as it is written, 'There shall come out of Sion the Deliverer, and shall turn away ungodliness from Jacob'," Rom11:26, quoting Is59:20-21. The same power that delivered Israel out of Egypt, is the same power that delivers us from bondage to Sin. Note well the statement that, "so all Israel shall be saved". How shall all Israel be saved? By the coming in of the Gentiles. Then will Israel be full, and the blindness will have passed away!! Christ, the Deliverer, turns away ungodliness from Jacob, by saving Gentile sinners as well as sinners of the Jews. God's covenant is for all. The forgiveness of sins and Christ's righteousness to straighten us out contemplate the preparation to meet Him. "For this is My Covenant unto them, when I shall take away their sins," Rom11:27.

The Gentiles who believe in Christ experience an enemy status so far as the Jews are concerned. Rom11:28: "As concerning the Gospel, they are enemies for your sakes: but as touching the election, they are beloved for the fathers' sakes." Nevertheless, God's "election" of the Jews in His everlasting covenant, has not been revoked. It was that covenant promise which He gave to their patriarchs. St Paul supports his point by blending ideas found in Is59:20-21; 27:9; and Jer31:33-34: "As it is written: 'The Deliverer will come out of Zion; He will remove ungodliness from Jacob. And this is My Covenant with them, when I take away their sins'," Rom11:26-27. Isaiah says, "A protector comes to Zion, to those in Jacob who repent of their rebellious deeds," and Jeremiah promises a new covenant in which God will not remember their sins any more.

St Paul knows that the Redeemer has come to Zion — Jesus has come, and St Paul is confident that Jesus will accomplish the work He came to do. Even when the nation was a mess, God used the prophets to promise a Day of Salvation for them, and He promised a New Covenant for them. The fact that Gentiles are entering the New Covenant does not change the fact that it was promised to Israel. The promise is not broken — rather, it is expanded to include Gentiles. The Redeemer not only came to Zion, but He is now going out from Zion to save Gentiles.

"Concerning the Gospel they are enemies for your sake, but concerning the election they are beloved for the sake of the fathers," Rom11:28. St Paul gives us his summary and conclusion in this verse. Most of the Jews are enemies of the Gospel, but God still loves them, and they are still part of the chosen people. Why? "For the gifts and the call of God are irrevocable," Rom11:29. God will keep

His promises. When will all this happen? St Paul does not say. The Jews can turn to Christ at any time. The salvation in Christ which God has given in the Covenant and God's effectual calling of every Jew by name is continuous and unrelenting, but not irresistible. God has not rolled over on His promise.

"For as you were once disobedient to God, yet have now obtained mercy through their disobedience, even so these also have now been disobedient, that through the mercy shown you they also may obtain mercy. For God has committed them all to disobedience, that He might have mercy on all," RomII:30-32.

Historically, you Gentiles were classified "non-believers". For as you in times past have not believed God, yet have now obtained mercy through their unbelief. Presently, the Jewish classification as "non-believers" means good to you Gentiles so you may partake of "the root and fatness" of Christ and fill out the good olive tree. St Paul summarizes it in Rom11:30-31. It is still God's purpose to change the status of Jewish "non-believers" into "believers". So, the bottom line as far as God is concerned is that we are all, both Jew and Gentile, born into this world in a state of unbelief. "For God has committed them all to disobedience, that He might have mercy upon all," Rom11:32.

Mercy is given to Gentiles; it is also given to Jews, for salvation is by Grace. Mercy is undeserved and unmerited, but nonetheless given stingily to souls in desperate need. It is God's mercy that gives faith to all. Since God does not have a merit system, it is by His gift and not an offer that we are saved. Everyone has sinned and deserves a guilty verdict, but in Christ all are given mercy. The Grace of God is "bringing salvation to all people" (Tts2:11) — to all races and nations.

St Cyril of Alexandria: St Paul shows that both Jews and Gentiles were guilty of the same thing and that they were likewise cleansed by one and the same Grace.

Of all judgments, spiritual judgments are the sorest; of these the apostle is here speaking. The restoration of the Jews is, in the course of things, far less improbable than the call of the Gentiles to be the children of Abraham;

and though others now possess these privileges (being the children of Abraham), it will not hinder their being admitted again. By rejecting the Gospel, and by their indignation at its being preached to the Gentiles, the Jews have become enemies to God; yet they are still to be favoured for the sake of their pious Fathers (Rom11:28). Though at present they are enemies to the Gospel, for their hatred to the Gentiles; yet, when God's time is come, that will no longer exist, and God's love to their Fathers will be remembered.

True Grace seeks not to confine God's favour. Those who find mercy themselves, should endeavour that through their mercy others also may obtain mercy. Not that the Jews will be restored to have their priesthood, and temple, and ceremonies again; an end is put to all these. But they are to be brought to believe in Christ; they become one sheep-fold with the Gentiles, under Christ the Great Shepherd. The captivities of Israel, their dispersion, and their being shut out from the Church, are emblems of the believer's corrections for doing wrong. The continued care of the Lord towards that people, and the final mercy and blessed restoration intended for them, show the patience and love of God.

ISRAEL'S ROLE

Has God rejected His people? St Paul's answer was unequivocal: "May it never be!" Rom11:1. Indeed, the 11th chapter of Romans is St Paul's treatise on the role and future of Israel in God's plan of redemption. The apostle St Paul reasserts what was the clear teaching of the Old Testament (Jer31:31-34; Ezk36:24-28, 37:21-28; Hos3:4-5; Joel 3:16-21; Zec10:6-12, 12:10). God is not through with Israel, and He has a grand plan for their future. St Paul, when speaking of the Church's relationship to Israel, he speaks of us as being "grafted in" (Rom11:17), "brought near" (Eph2:13), "descendants of Abraham by faith" (Rom4:16), "heirs" of Abraham's promise (Gal 3:29), and as "sharing" in Israel's blessings (Rom15:27).

St Paul then says: "For I do not desire, brethren, that you should be ignorant of this Mystery, lest you should be wise in your own opinion, that blindness in part has happened to Israel until the fullness of the Gentiles has come in," Rom11:25.

The blindness of Israel is a mystery because it explains the unbelief of so many Jews and how the Gentiles are now being united to the remnant of the faithful Jews; thus, this body of believers together form the true Israel. In Gal 6:15-16, St Paul calls those "in Christ Jesus" the "Israel of God", which is the Church. This true Israel is not based on biological ancestry but on faithfulness to God's Deliverer, the Messiah. In this understanding, all Israel will be saved (Rom11:26).

The New Covenant inaugurated by Jesus in the upper room with His disciples, is the same New Covenant spoken of in the book of Jeremiah (Jer31:31), and the only covenant mentioned by the New Testament. Because of God's Grace and His plan to extend His blessing to all peoples, we have been included with the Jews into the New Covenant.

THE MYSTERY OF THE
RESURRECTION OF THE DEAD

It is a mystery since it is not necessary for all of us to die. Some will be alive when Jesus returns. The living shall be changed. "And we shall be changed," 1Co15:52, proving that the resurrection body is different, yet likely similar to our present bodies.

"Now this I say, brethren, that flesh and blood cannot inherit the kingdom of God; nor does corruption inherit incorruption. Behold, I tell you a mystery: We shall not all sleep, but we shall all be changed — in a moment, in the twinkling of an eye, at the last trumpet. For the trumpet will sound, and the dead will be raised incorruptible, and we shall be changed. For this corruptible must put on incorruption, and this mortal must put on immortality. So when this corruptible has put on incorruption, and this mortal has put on immortality, then shall be brought to pass the saying that is written: "Death is swallowed up in victory." "O Death, where is your sting? O Hades, where is your victory?" The sting of death is sin, and the strength of sin is the law. But thanks be to God, who gives us the

The Mystery Of The Resurrection Of The Dead

victory through our Lord Jesus Christ.

Therefore, my beloved brethren, be steadfast, immovable, always abounding in the work of the Lord, knowing that your labour is not in vain in the Lord," ICol5:50-58.

"But I do not want you to be ignorant, brethren, concerning those who have fallen asleep, lest you sorrow as others who have no hope. For if we believe that Jesus died and rose again, even so God will bring with Him those who sleep in Jesus. For this we say to you by the word of the Lord, that we who are alive and remain until the coming of the Lord will by no means precede those who are asleep. For the Lord Himself will descend from heaven with a shout, with the voice of an archangel, and with the trumpet of God. And the dead in Christ will rise first. Then we who are alive and remain shall be caught up together with them in the clouds to meet the Lord in the air. And thus we shall always be with the Lord," ITh4:13-17.

The verses in 1Co15:50-58 and 1Th4:13-17 give us a little insight into a future event known as "The Rapture". While this word itself does not appear in the Bible, the event is real nonetheless. We get the word "Rapture" from the Latin translation of the Greek word "arpazw" (harpazo). It means just what the King James Bible says it does, "caught up". The rapture is that future event when the Lord Jesus Himself will return in the clouds above this earth in His Second Coming.

One common theme that punctuates each of these references is the mention of the "trumpet". We are told in clear language that the Rapture will be a time that will be heralded with the sound of trumpets. When the writers of the New Testament used the imagery of trumpets, the people to whom they were writing were well acquainted with what they were saying. However, we modern readers need to be educated about the significance of the trumpet.

In the Bible, trumpets were used for four specific purposes:
- To proclaim victoryTo Call an Assembly
- To announce a warning
- To call the troops to battle

It is clear to see how the trumpets fit with the idea of the rapture. All four of these events will take place when the rapture comes about:

- Victory over the world will be announced by the Church.
- The dead and the living will be called to assemble themselves in the presence of the Lord.
- The trumpets will announce a warning of judgment to the world.
- The angelic troops will be summoned to battle.

Also, in the society of that day, trumpets were heard on a daily basis. The Roman army, which occupied most of the civilized world at that time used trumpets to carry out the movement of their troops. Typically, when a Roman legion moved, there would be three blasts from the trumpets. The first would tell the troop to strike their tents and to prepare to move. The second would alert them to fall in and line up. The last trumpet would be the signal to move out. Notice what St Paul says in 1Co15:52. He tells us that we are leaving at the "last trump". When the trumpet sounds, it will be the signal to move up to glory!

WHEN TRUMPETS FADE

Before the sound of that trumpet blast fades from our ears, several great and precious events will take place.

Our Lord Will Have Returned

In fulfilment of His promise: Before the Lord Jesus went to the Cross, He promised His disciples that He would return for them one day (Jn14:1-3). He later reaffirmed this promise to the apostle John (Rev22:20). Just as sure as there is a blue sky above us He will return as He promised He would! Even as He was ascending back into Heaven, angelic messengers were dispatched to tell the apostles of the Lord's impending return.

"And when he had spoken these things, while they beheld, he was taken up; and a cloud received him out of their sight. And while they looked steadfastly toward heaven as he went up, behold, two men stood by them in white apparel; Which also said, Ye men of Galilee, why stand ye gazing up into heaven? this same Jesus, which is taken up from you into heaven, shall so come in like manner as ye have seen him go into heaven," Acts1:9-11,

In fulfilment of His purpose: While the Lord was making His promise to return some day, He also stated His purpose. "And if I go and prepare a place for you, I will come again and receive you to Myself; that where I am, there you may be also," Jn14:3. The Lord desires to receive His bride unto Himself (Eph5:25-27). After all, He paid the ultimate price to redeem her from her sins and to cleanse her from her filthiness! He died on the cross to purchase His Bride and He wants her to be with Him in His heavenly home.

All Departed Will Have Been Resurrected

Their present condition: "But I do not want you to be ignorant, brethren, concerning those who have fallen asleep, lest you sorrow as others who have no hope,"1Th4:13. Those saints who have departed are "asleep". This does not refer to "soul sleep". It refers to the fact that their bodies are asleep. When the saints of God leave this world, their souls are immediately ushered into the presence of the Lord. This was the conviction St Paul held. "We are confident, I say, and willing rather to be absent from the body, and to be present with the Lord," 2Co5:8. "For I am hard-pressed between the two, having a desire to depart, and to be with Christ; which is far better," Php1:23. Presently, all those who left this world in a saved condition are in the presence of the Lord Jesus Christ.

Their promised completion: "For the trumpet will sound, and the dead will be raised incorruptible, and we shall be changed," 1Co15:52b. All the departed will be raised "incorruptible". That is, they will be changed! When they left their body, it was destined for the ground from which it came. However, when the Lord Jesus returns, He will bring their spirits back with Him, He will raise their bodies and glorify them. He will then place the spirits back into those newly glorified bodies! The living body must put on incorruption, and immortality (1Co15:53). The wicked dead will rise with eternal, incorruptible bodies, but likely minus the glorious aspect of the bodies of the saints (Is66:23, 24).

HOW WILL ALL THIS HAPPEN?

Certainly, to our mortal minds it is a great mystery. However, if you take the time to look back at the times our Lord shouted while He was on this earth, you will discover

The Mystery Of The Resurrection Of The Dead 151

that each time He did so, dead folks got out of their graves. He shouted in Bethany and Lazarus lived! (Jn11:43-44). He shouted at Calvary and some lived! (Mt27:50-52). He will shout from the clouds and all the departed saints will live (1Th4:16). There is power is the Word of our Lord!

Suddenly: The events following His return will not happen over a long period of time, but all of a sudden. "In a moment, in the twinkling of an eye, at the last trumpet. For the trumpet will sound, and the dead will be raised incorruptible, and we shall be changed," 1Co15:52. Notice the use of words that imply speed and swiftness. "Moment" speaks of an "indivisible point in time. A span of time so short that there is none shorter"; "twinkling of an eye": Scientists have determined that the blink of an eye is 1/30th of a second in duration. That is fast! However, a twinkling is event faster than that, somewhere in the neighbourhood of 1000th of a second!

Then in 1Th4:17, St Paul uses the term "caught up". This phrase means "to snatch away, to seize with force, to claim for oneself." It refers to a sudden event when the saints of God will be "snatched from this world with force and claimed for the glory of God." "Then we who are alive and remain shall be caught up together with them in the clouds to meet the Lord in the air. And thus we shall always be with the Lord," 1Th4:17.

The whole idea here is one of speed! There will be no forewarning. There will be no announcements on Facebook, TV, radio, or in the papers. There will be no announcements from the pulpits. It will just happen! My friend, if you have ever listened to anything in your life, then listen to this. You need to be ready! Jesus Himself said, "Therefore you also be ready: for the Son of man is coming at an hour you do not expect," Mt24:44.

If He were to come today, would He find you ready? Oh friend, do not be deceived, it could happen! Today could be that glorious day when the Lord returns for His people. Will you be in that number that hears the shout, that hears the trumpets and that leaves this world in an instant? Only if you are born again! Be ready, He is coming!

"For the trumpet will sound, and the dead will be raised incorruptible, and we shall be changed. For this corruptible must put on incorruption, and this mortal must put on immortality. So when this corruptible has put on incorruption, and this mortal has put on immortality, then shall be brought to pass the saying that is written: "Death is swallowed up in victory." "O Death, where is your sting? O Hades, where is your victory?" The sting of death is sin, and the strength of sin is the Law. But thanks be to God, who gives us the victory through our Lord Jesus Christ," ICo15:52b-57.

Changed Physically: At the moment of the rapture, all the saints will experience a radical change. These mortal bodies will be changed to immortal ones. The bodies that are not destined to perish will be made like the body of our Lord. A body that cannot experience death, decay or disease. A body that will shine with the brilliance of 10,000 suns. What a day that will be!

Changed Perfectly: When this change comes, it will remake us into the image of our glorified Lord. "Beloved,

now are we the sons of God, and it doth not yet appear what we shall be: but we know that, when he shall appear, we shall be like Him; for we shall see Him as He is," 1Jn3:2. We do not know a lot about our Lord's glorified body, but we do know that:

- It is a body not bound by time or space (Jn20:19).
- It is a body that can enjoy food and fellowship (Lk24:36-43).
- It is a body that can never die (Heb7:25).
- It is a body that shines with a heavenly brilliance (Rev21:23; Mt17:2).

All of this is enough to let me know that I want one of these bodies someday. All the saints will wear a glorified body when we arrive in that Heavenly home!

Changed permanently: The language of our texts tells us that we will no longer be mortal. These new bodies will never wear down or wear out, but they will last throughout eternity. They will be a perfect in 10,000,000 years as they were the day we received them! Notice what St Paul says about this body, "For we know that if our earthly house this tent, is destroyed, we have a building from God, a house not made with hands, eternal in the heavens," 2Co5:1.

United with our loved ones: "Then we who are alive and remain shall be caught up together with them in the clouds to meet the Lord in the air. And thus, we shall always be with the Lord," 1Th4:13-17. Notice the phrase "together with them in the clouds". This indicates that all the children of God will be together forever in Heaven. Imagine being reunited with spouses, parents, children and grandparents. Imagine seeing your departed loved ones in their new glorified bodies in the presence of the Lord Jesus! What a glorious privilege has been given to all the saints of God!

Met with Our Lord: As great as that reunion with our loved ones will be, it will be eclipsed by another reunion. This same verse tells us that "so shall we ever be with the Lord."

My friends, one day, we will see Him Who died for us on the Cross! We will look at His face. We will be able to bow before Him in adoration and worship. We will be in the presence of the Lord Jesus Christ! I can imagine no thrill any greater in this universe than to see the One Who loved me enough to lay down His life in payment for my own. Hallelujah! Just the thought of that is enough to make a Christian shout! Glory! Glory!

 Have you ever come to the place where you knew you were lost? Have you repented and confessed your sins? Have you placed your faith in the death and resurrection of the Lord Jesus Christ? Have you received Christ as your personal Saviour?

THE JUDGMENT

Because Adam sinned, all must die. Because Christ rose, all must rise to be judged. "And as it is appointed unto men once to die, but after this the judgment," Heb9:27. God has appointed His Son Jesus Christ to be the judge of all earth. "For we must all appear before the judgment seat of Christ," 2Co5:10. The judgment of the believers will take place in the air, immediately following the general resurrection at the Second Coming of Christ (1Th4:13-17). "For the Son of man shall come in the glory of His Father with His angels, and then He shall reward every man according to his works," Mt16:27.

Christians will be judged in respect of their stewardship of the talents, gifts, opportunities and responsibilities granted to them during the course of their lives. While all will enjoy perfect bliss, there will be degrees also in the enjoyment of heaven (2Co9:6). The believer's sins committed and confessed after conversion will not be judged (1Jn1:9); confessed sin is forgiven and cleansed forever.

WHAT THEN WILL WE BE JUDGED FOR?

- Our works will be judged. "Every man's work shall be made manifest ... and the fire shall try every man's work of what sort it is," 1Co3:13. "For God shall bring every work into judgment" Ecc12:14.
- Our words: "That every idle word that men speak, they shall give account thereof in the day of judgment," Mt12:36, 37.
- Our thoughts: "For out of the heart proceed evil thoughts ....; these are the things which defile a man ...," Mt15:19, 20; also, ".... looks .... lust......," Mt5:28.
- Our secrets: "In the day when God shall judge the secrets of men by Jesus Christ according to my Gospel," Rom2:16.
- Our motives: Correct motives, "constrained by His love," 1Co5:14. Wrong motives, self-glory. "Therefore let no man glory in men," 1Co3:21.

The test will be by fire. "For the day shall declare it, because it shall be revealed by fire; and the fire shall try every man's work of what sort it is," 1Co3:13. This will be a fair impartial public display of justice. No one will be able to say that God showed favouritism. "Be not deceived; God is not mocked: for whatsoever man sows, that shall he also reap," Gal 6:7,

Any day we could meet the Lord, either because He has returned, or because we have passed away. None of us should take life for granted. Jesus said, "I am coming and My reward is with Me, to render every man according to what he has done," Rev22:12. Christians then live vigilantly like servants who daily expect the return of their master (Lk12:35-38).

Thrice-holy God, Who with Your infinite love created and sustain us, You admire and bless us whenever we do good, You tolerate us when we sin, You forgive us when we repent. You deigned that Your only begotten Son should become man, to be crucified, to die as a man, to be resurrected and become the first-born from the dead, and to make possible our own resurrection. We thank You for all these things. We ask You please to give us repentance. Make it so that we will proceed to the resurrection of life and not to judgement. Grant us eternal life. Do not allow our eternal punishment. Do not deprive us of the joy of Your everlasting presence.

CONTRARY TO SCRIPTURES

There is a strange belief in the Rapture which teaches that someday (sooner rather than later), without warning, born-again Christians will begin to float up from the freeway, abandoned vehicles careening wildly. There will be airliners in the sky suddenly with no one at the controls! Presumably, God is removing these favoured ones from earth to spare them the tribulation of the Anti-Christ which the rest of us will have to endure.

The Rapture represents a radical misinterpretation of Scripture. The Rapture is mistakenly thought as Christian doctrine. It is not! It is a serious distortion of Scripture. According to the Bible and according to the belief not only of Orthodox Christians but also of the Roman Catholic and most Protestant Mainline Churches, the true Rapture will not be secret; it will be the great and very visible Second Coming of Jesus at the end of the world. That is the one and only "Rapture". It will not be a separate, secret event but one that every eye shall see (1Th4:16-17).

The word rapture is not found in Scripture but some translations refer to it where St Paul says that when the Lord comes again "we who are alive...shall be caught up... in the clouds to meet the Lord in the air," 1Th4:17. This "being caught up...in the clouds" — "arpagisometha" in Greek, is translated by some as "raptured". The word itself is not found in Orthodox theology.

The notion of a rapture in which Christ comes unseen to take believers away secretly, and only later comes back again for everyone else publicly — this whole teaching is quite novel. It was almost unheard of until John Nelson Darby formulated it in the 1800s as part of a new approach to the Bible, sometimes called "dispensationalism".

The purpose of the "Rapture" is to protect the elect from the tribulations of the end times. Yet Jesus said nothing about sparing anyone from tribulation. In fact, He said, "In the world you have tribulation, but be of good cheer. I have overcome the world."

The Mystery Of The Resurrection Of The Dead

Nowhere did Jesus ever say that He would return secretly to rapture the elect. Rather, He promised to be with His elect in all tribulations. "Lo, I am with you always. I will never leave you or forsake you." He even had something good to say about being persecuted: "Blessed are those who are persecuted for righteousness' sake, for theirs is the kingdom of heaven," Mt5:10.

Those who espouse the Rapture claim that Mt24:40-41 refers clearly to the rapture of the just, "Then shall two be in the field; the one shall be taken, and the other left. Two women shall be grinding at the mill; the one shall be taken, and the other left." The entire passage, however, refers to Christ's Second Coming where He will judge the living and the dead and separate the just from the unjust.

Darby taught as dogma that when the Scriptures reveal that the Lord will reign on earth for a thousand years (Rev20:4), this figure is to be taken literally, rather than as a symbol for eternity as we believe. The Council of Ephesus in 431 AD condemned as heresy this teaching which is called "chialiasmos" (millennialism or 1000 years).

In fact, the Ecumenical Councils in which the essential

truths of the Christian faith were defined never mention a rapture. Yet evangelical Christians and Pentecostals keep using obscure passages of the Book of Revelation which purport to give a detailed timetable of what will happen at the end of the world, despite the fact that Jesus Himself warned that no man knows either the day or the hour when the Son of Man shall return.

A major problem with the Rapture is that it ends up teaching not two but three comings of Jesus — first His birth in Bethlehem; second, His secret coming to snatch away (rapture) the "born-again"; and third, His coming at the end of the world to judge the living and the dead and to reign in glory. Yet only two not three comings of Christ are mentioned in the Bible. We have the clearest definition of this in the Nicene Creed when we confess that "the Lord Jesus Christ...will come again in glory to judge the living and the dead. His Kingdom will have no end.... I expect the resurrection of the dead. And the life of the ages to come." There is no mention of a "Rapture".

As already stated, most Christians, Orthodox, Roman Catholics and Protestants do not believe in the Rapture. In fact, one Protestant pastor, John L. Bray, summarized magnificently what we Orthodox and most other

Christians believe about the Rapture when he wrote these remarkable words:

"Though many believe and teach this "Pre-Tribulation Rapture" theory, they erroneously do so, because neither Jesus, St Paul, St Peter, St John, nor any of the other writers of the Bible taught this. Nor did the early Church fathers, nor any others for many hundreds of years.... Did you know that none of this was ever taught prior to 1812, and that all forms of Pre-Tribulation Rapture teaching were developed since that date? .... If I were to preach something, or believe something, supposedly from the Bible, but cannot find that anyone else before 1812 ever believed it or taught it, I would seriously question that it is based on the Bible," John L Bray.

Thus, the Rapture is foreign to the Bible and to the living tradition of the Church. It is what we call a heresy, a false teaching. False teachings, such as this, happen when people — like John Darby — believe that they have the right to interpret the Scriptures individually apart from the Living Body of Christ — the Church — where the Spirit of Truth abides and leads us to all truth.

Jesus speaks of the one and only "Rapture", the Second Coming: "Be on guard. Be alert! You do not know when that time will come...keep watch...if he comes suddenly, do not let Him find you sleeping. What I say to you, I say to everyone: Watch!" Mk13:32-37.

When it comes to Christianity, the "faith once delivered to the saints" (Jude 1:3), there is a simple rule: "if it's new, it just can't be true!"

GOD'S COMING KINGDOM

The hope of Christians is focused on the permanent values of God's Coming Kingdom. Jesus has prepared an eternal home for each believer. He promised, "In My Father's house are many mansions.... I go to prepare a place for you. And if I go and prepare a place for you I will come again and receive you to Myself; that where I am, there you may be also," Jn14:2, 3.

The Church looks forward to the coming of Christ on the Last Day of Judgement to hear the blessed words of the King, "Come, you blessed of My Father, inherit the kingdom prepared for you from the foundation of the world," Mt25:34. As Christians, we don't have to be anxious about bad news. No matter what happens on earth, we can take comfort in knowing that we have eternal life. The Holy Spirit will empower us to do whatever the Father asks of us. And Scripture promises peace if we will give our worries to God and trust in Him.

The return of Christ is a comfort not a threat. "Therefore, comfort one another with these words," 1Th4:18. At present, at the end of reciting the Creed, we sing in a joyful tune: "we wait for the resurrection of the dead and the life to come". We happily look forward to the next life, when all righteous Christians will be transformed into Christ's image and attain full eschatological life beyond the reach of death. Then our salvation will be complete (Rom8:25, 2Cor3:18).

As we anticipate our Lord's return, we will pay attention to our lifestyles. The choices we make should be testimonies to those who don't believe. Thus, St Paul writes, "denying ungodliness and worldly lusts, we should live soberly, righteously, and Godly in the present age, looking for the blessed hope and glorious appearing of our great God and Saviour Jesus Christ, who gave Himself for us, that He might redeem us from every lawless deed and purify for Himself His own special people, zealous for good works," Tts2:12-14.

God's timing is not ours. Regardless of when Christ's return is, we should seek to follow His will for our lives. Do you actively invest your life in seeking and obeying the will of God? I pray that you will evaluate your thoughts, activities and priorities in light of Christ's return. Jesus could appear at any moment. Will you be ready?

"Amen, even so, come Lord Jesus," Rev22:20.

"Maranatha, the Lord is near," 1Co16:22.

THE MYSTERY OF INIQUITY

"Now, brethren, concerning the coming of our Lord Jesus Christ and our gathering together to Him, we ask you, not to be soon shaken in mind or troubled, either by spirit or by word or by letter, as if from us, as though the day of Christ had come. Let no one deceive you by any means; for that Day will not come unless the falling away comes first, and the man of sin is revealed, the son of perdition, who opposes and exalts himself above all that is called God or that is worshiped, so that he sits as God in the temple of God, showing himself that he is God.

Do you not remember that when I was still with you I told you these things? And now you know what is restraining, that he may be revealed in his own time. For the mystery of lawlessness is already at work; only He who now restrains will do so until He is taken out of the way. And then the lawless one will be revealed, whom the Lord will consume with the breath of His mouth and destroy with the brightness of His coming. The coming of the lawless one is according to the working of

Satan, with all power, signs, and lying wonders," ITh2:1-9.

The Orthodox Church believes that there are many antichrists who came and will come into the world as false prophets and teachers who bring in destructive heresies, and many will follow their destructive ways (2Pt2:1-2). St John spoke about those heretics, who deny the divinity of the Lord and His Incarnation for the salvation of mankind and calls them "antichrists and liars, who deny the Father and the Son" (1Jn2:18-22). The Church tells the believers that they must not receive them in their houses nor greet them, as advised by St John, in order not to share in their evil deeds (2Jn:9-11).

"And I saw an angel coming down out of heaven, having the key to the Abyss and holding in his hand a great chain. He seized the dragon, that ancient serpent, who is the devil, or Satan, and bound him for a thousand years. He threw him into the Abyss, and locked and sealed it over him, to keep him from deceiving the nations anymore until the thousand years were ended. After that, he must be set free for a short time.

I saw thrones on which were seated those who had been given authority to judge. And I saw the souls of those who had been beheaded because of their testimony about Jesus and because of the word of God. They had not worshiped the beast or its image and had not received its mark on their foreheads or their hands. They came to life and reigned with Christ a thousand years. (The rest of the dead did not come to life until the thousand years were ended.) This is the first resurrection. Blessed and holy are those who share in the first resurrection. The second death has no power over them, but they will be priests of God and of Christ and will reign with him for a thousand years," Rev 20:1-6.

THE MILLENNIUM CONCEPTS

The millennium is the thousand-year era described at the end of the book of Revelation (Rev20:1-6). It is interpreted as the Church age when Jesus reigns on earth in those who believe. According to the Orthodox teaching, the millennium is the period between the First and Second Comings of Our Lord Jesus Christ.

Much of modern Christendom has succumbed to divisive speculation regarding Christ's return. We are divided into pre-millennial, post-millennial and a-millennial camps. Breaking it down even further, there are pre-tribulation, mid-tribulation, and post-tribulation adherents. Christians part away and new denominations spring up around interpretations of events which have not yet even come to pass!

But these expectations of when the millennium will occur reflect far more important beliefs within each system about how the millennium will occur – that is, about what, if anything, will create such an era.

Premillennialism is the belief that Christ's return will be pre-millennial, that is, it will precede the millennium. Premillennialism is more accurately the belief that Christ's return will be required to bring about the millennium, because nothing short of this will be sufficient. In this view, the kingdom of God is an eschatological reality that comes over against history.

Postmillennialism is the belief that Christ's coming will be post-millennial, that is, it will follow this millennium. Postmillennialism, by contrast to Premillennialism, is the belief that Christ's return will come as the culmination of the millennium, because it will have been brought about previously by inner-historical forces such as the progress of literacy, education, charity, etc.; the advancement of the influence of the gospel on culture; or similar things. In this view, the kingdom of God is a historical reality that comes within history.

Amillennialism is the belief that Christ's coming will be without a millennium, that is, that there will be no world-wide era of peace and justice at the end of history. Amillennialism, for its part, is the belief that Christ's return will take place without a millennium, since from this perspective God does not intend to bring about a worldwide era of peace and justice on earth. In this view, the kingdom of God is a spiritual reality that comes apart from history.

According to the Orthodox Church, Christ's Kingdom is "not of this world" (Jn18.31). He says this to Pontius Pilate when being mocked as king, revealing in this humiliation His genuine divine kingship. The Kingdom of God, which Christ will rule, will come with power at the end of time when the Lord will fill all creation and will be truly "all, and in all" (Col 3.11). The Church, which in popular Orthodox doctrine is called the Kingdom of God on earth, has already mysteriously been given this experience. In the Church, Christ is already acknowledged, glorified, and served, as the only King and Lord; and His Holy Spirit, whom the saints of the Church have identified with the Kingdom of God, is already given to the world in the Church with full graciousness and power.

The Kingdom of God, therefore, is a Divine Reality. It is the reality of God's presence among men through Christ and the Holy Spirit. "For the Kingdom of God . . . means . . . peace and joy and righteousness in the Holy Spirit" (Rom14:17). The Kingdom of God as a spiritual, divine reality is given to men by Christ in the Church. It is celebrated and participated in the sacramental mysteries of the faith. It is witnessed to in the Scriptures, the Ecumenical Councils, the Canons, and the saints. It will become the universal, final cosmic reality for the whole of creation at the end of the ages when Christ comes in glory to fill all things with Himself by the Holy Spirit, that God might be "all and in all" (1Co15:28).

THE LAWLESS ONE

While we are warned against predicting the Day of the Lord (Mt24:36; Acts1:7; 1Th5:1), there will be signs preceding His Coming. St Paul instructs the Thessalonians concerning two such signs (2Th2:3):

- A general "falling away" from Christ and the Church (apostasy); and
- The revealing of "the man of sin, the son of perdition" who is the antichrist of 1 and 2 John, similar to the dragon and the beast of Revelation 13.

St Paul says that the antichrist will come after the falling away, clarifying that he is "the man of sin, the son of perdition, who opposes and exalts himself above all that is called God or that is worshipped, so that he sits as God in the temple of God, showing that he is God," 2Th2:3-4.

This lawless one is described in the Old Testament (Dan7:25; 8:25; 11:36), mentioned by Christ (Mt24:15), and discussed by St Paul on his first visit to Thessalonica (2Th2:5). The devil incites divisions among the people so they will readily receive the antichrist when he comes. The man of sin is a counterfeit messiah with a counterfeit kingdom.

This lawless one exalts himself above God (2Th2:4). St Paul also refers to the reality of spiritual opposition in 2Th2:7-10. In this passage, he again uses the word "mystery". In the context of this passage, it is clear that St Paul is talking about the Second Coming of Christ. In line with that usage, "the mystery of lawlessness" is likely a reference to the satanic opposition he mentions in 2Th2:9: "the one whose coming is in accord with the activity of Satan".

"For the mystery of lawlessness is already at work; only He who now restrains will do so until He is taken out of the way. And then the lawless one will be revealed, whom the Lord will consume with the breath of His mouth and destroy with the brightness of His coming. The coming of the lawless one is according to the working of Satan, with all power, signs, and lying wonders, and with all unrighteous deception among those who perish, because they did not receive the love of the truth, that they might be saved," 2Th2:7-10.

If we read through the whole passage (2Th2:7-10), we will see that the flow of the passage is about Satan at work, and a major manifestation and goal of satanic activity is lawlessness and the promotion of lawlessness. God wants us to know that perceiving the role of Satan is essential for an accurate understanding of the manifestations of lawlessness.

Although the evil one has always been at work to promote lawlessness and wickedness, in the last days, this will be intensified. This is a reality we have to bear in mind as we seek to be faithful to God and serve Him well in the last days.

So, St Paul is saying here that the mystery of lawlessness is already at work, and behind it is Satan. But there is a restraining factor. "Only He who now restrains will do so until He is taken out of the way" (2Th2:7). The evil one and what he is seeking to do is being restrained until the One who is restraining is taken out of the way. Then that "lawless one" will be revealed. The lawless one is likely to be a reference to the anti-Christ. The manifestation and activity of the lawless one, the anti-Christ, will be a significant event and strategy of Satan in his opposition to God's purposes.

This lawless one will be removed from power by Christ Himself at His Second Coming (2Th2:8). Through the anti-Christ, Satan will seek to promote lawlessness, wickedness and deception in the last days. What he will do is revealed in greater detail in the Book of Revelation. When Christ appears again, He will slay the lawless one, the anti-Christ, with the breath of His mouth (2Th2:8).

He performs deceptive miracles and wonders through satanic power (2Th2:9). "The coming of the lawless one will be according to the working of Satan, with all the power, signs, and lying wonders, and with all the unrighteous deception among those who perish, because they did not receive the love of the truth, that they might be saved," 2Th2:9-10. This tells us that a major strategy the evil one uses to tear down God's work is deception. It is important therefore that we understand the strategy of the evil one and learn how to counter him.

He will fool the unrighteous into following him (2Th2:10-12). He added that the lawless one will be revealed whom the Lord will consume with the breath of His mouth and destroy with the brightness of His coming.

The Church believes that the antichrist that will appear

in the last days before the Second Coming of the Lord is the beast that will come from the sea as mentioned in Revelation 13 and interpreted by many forefathers. On the other hand, the book of Revelation tells us that the false prophet is the beast who will rise up from the earth (Rev13:11). Both the antichrist and the false prophet work together through demons.

St Andrew of Caesarea and St Victorinus of Petovium: The false prophet is the armour bearer of the antichrist and by sorcery and deceit will prepare the way for the antichrist. He will be full of malice and he does the work of the devil.

The Book of Revelation gives examples of his remarkable signs, such as making fire fall from heaven and his servants will speak multiple tongues, as if they received the gift of the Holy Spirit, with fiery tongues as the disciples of the Lord Jesus (Rev13:13).

Irenaeus: The antichrist would perform the miracles by ways of magic and not by divine power.

By God's permission, he will do amazing things in order to delude the souls of God's children, that he would be accepted by them instead of Christ. Thus, "All the world marvelled and followed the beast," Rev13:3.

The name of the antichrist is not given in the Book of Revelation, but the number of that beast "is a human number, and it is 666," Rev13:18. Although many scholars tried to know his name, according to many calculations, the Orthodox Church advises the believers not to attempt to know his name. He is, in any case full of shame and wickedness.

As St John the Baptist led those who believed to the Saviour, this false prophet will deceive many into believing that the antichrist is "God" (Rev13:4). The antichrist will deceive many people, rule everything (one world government), and will persecute the Church and all those who do not obey him (Rev13:12-17).

But for those who will suffer for the sake of their

Christian belief, their reward will be the heavenly citizenship and the inheritance of the Kingdom of God. St Paul instructs that when the world gets worse, Christians must not be distressed or deceived (2Th2:11), but rather persevere as good stewards (2Th2:13-17).

THE MYSTERY OF THE BRIDE OF CHRIST

Biblical metaphors allow us to understand more clearly the mysteries of God. For example, when St Paul spoke of the relationship between a husband and wife, his purpose was to reveal a deeper "mystery". The relationship a husband has with his wife is supposed to model a spiritual truth concerning Christ and His church.

In ancient Near Eastern culture, parents typically chose a wife for their son and arranged for the marriage by legal contract. It was then the responsibility of the father of the bride-to-be to ensure his daughter's virginity during the betrothal period. Betrothal was considered almost as binding as marriage itself. The betrothed couple addressed each other as "wife" and "husband" (Dt22:23-24; Joel 1:8), and sexual faithfulness was expected.

This mystery is great: As a wife is to her husband, so the Church is to Christ. The new birth at Baptism is the betrothal and Christ's return is the consummation of the marriage, when the Church will be presented as a pure virgin to her Groom.

THE CHURCH IS THE BRIDE OF CHRIST

Israel as the betrothed of Yahweh is a familiar theme in the Old Testament (Is54:5; 62:5; Ezk16:9-22; 23:27; Hos2:16-20). In the New Testament the bride-to-be is the Church and the groom is Christ (Mk2:18-22).

"The disciples of John and of the Pharisees were fasting. Then they came and said to Him, "Why do the disciples of John and of the Pharisees fast, but Your disciples do not fast?" And Jesus said to them, "Can the friends of the bridegroom fast while the bridegroom is with them? As long as they have the bridegroom with them they cannot fast. But the days will come when the bridegroom will be taken away from them, and then they will fast in those days," Mk2:18-20.

The first person to picture Christ as a groom was St John the Baptist (Jn3:29). As the forerunner of Christ, St John knew that he must decrease while Jesus must increase. In his understanding, Christ is a groom and His Bride is the messianic community. As the groom's friend,

St John rejoiced to attend the heavenly wedding feast where Jesus and His bride are united. Every marriage should be cause for celebration, but the marriage between Christ and His Church is something for the entire universe to celebrate for all eternity.

THE WEDDING FEAST

Jesus suggested a great marriage feast would be part of His final return to earth to be with His own. He used a number of direct and indirect references to this festive meal. The marriage supper was anticipated when Jesus celebrated the "Last Supper" with His disciples (Mt26:26-30).

The universality of God's invitation for all men everywhere to come to the marriage supper is clearly implied by a famous parable related by Jesus in Matthew 22. The required wedding garment represents true righteousness imparted by faith which replaces that normal self-righteous we all have as a result of the fall.

"And again Jesus spoke to them in parables, saying, 'The kingdom of heaven may be compared to a king who gave a marriage feast for his son, and sent his servants to call those who were invited to the marriage feast; but they would not come.... The wedding is ready, but those invited were not worthy. ...... For many are called, but few are chosen','" Mt22:1-14.

It is a great honour to be invited to this wedding feast. It is a feast to which the entire human race is invited, but only a fraction of the human race will attend. The invitation is the Gospel, and the Gospel has gone out to all men and women everywhere, in every age of history. Some accept the invitation. Some reject it. The Spirit of God has been calling men and women throughout the centuries, from Old Testament times through our own New Testament era and on into the future, even in the tribulation period. The invitation goes out to everyone: 'Come to the marriage feast of the Lamb!' What a privilege that will be, to see the Bridegroom face to face, to be a member of His Beloved Bride, to share in the intimacy of fellowship with the Lord Jesus!

The wedding feast celebration and intimate union with the Lord of the universe, who is Himself Love, will be so joyful, fulfilling and marvellous that all efforts should be focused on getting ready to attend.

Make sure you are one of the invited guests by trusting Christ's gift of salvation through simple faith in Him and His gracious work on the Cross that paid for the sins of all those who believe. Maranatha!

RELATIONSHIP BETWEEN HUSBAND AND WIFE

"Wives, submit to your own husbands, as to the Lord. For the husband is head of the wife, as also Christ is head of the church; and He is the Saviour of the body. Therefore, just as the Church is subject to Christ, so let the wives be to their own husbands in everything.

"Husbands, love your wives, just as Christ also loved the Church and gave Himself for her, that He might sanctify and cleanse her with the washing of water by the word, that He might present her to Himself a glorious church, not having spot or wrinkle or any such thing, but that she should be holy and without blemish. So husbands ought to love their own wives as their own bodies; he who loves his wife loves himself. For no one ever hated his own flesh, but nourishes and cherishes it, just as the Lord does the church. For we are members of His body, of His flesh and of His bones. 'For this reason a man shall leave his father and mother and be joined to his wife, and the two shall become one flesh.' This is a great mystery, but I speak concerning Christ and the Church," Eph5:22-33.

This passage (Eph5:22-33) is often referred to in messages on marriage and on husband and wife relationship. St Paul continued at length his moving portrayal of Christ's nuptial love for His Church. Like Christ, a husband is to care for his wife in the same way he cares for his own body, nourishing and cherishing her (Eph5:28-29). There is love between the husband, Christ, and His bride, the Church, with no hint of anything untoward or hateful.

Indeed, Eph5:22-33 is a passage very relevant to the subject of marriage. But this passage tells us something even more important than the relationship between husband and wife. It tells us what is in God's heart concerning the relationship between Christ and the Church and the fulfilment of God's purposes. If we understand the relationship between Christ and the Church, we will be able to better understand what the husband and wife relationship ought to be. In a way, the relationship between husbands and wives is supposed to mirror the relationship between Christ and the Church.

In Eph5:31, St Paul talks about oneness in the husband and wife relationship. He says that "a man shall leave his father and mother and shall be joined to his wife, and the two shall become one flesh" (Gn2:24). Then he concludes in Eph5:32 with this statement: "This mystery is great; but I am speaking with reference to Christ and the Church". That is, beyond the intimate love and oneness that God intends for the relationship between husband and wife, there is the intimate love and oneness in the relationship between Christ and the Church.

Marriage is a reflection of the magnificent mystery of union between Christ and His Church, completely unknown until the New Testament. A relationship of deep intimacy is suggested by the New Testament concept of the Church married to Christ. This mystery has to do with God's intention for the Church and the nature of the relationship between Christ and the Church. St Paul says: "This mystery is great. But I am speaking with reference to Christ and the Church." When St Paul says "this mystery is great", he is saying that this is indeed a marvellous and wonderful revelation. From this passage (Eph5:22-33), we can learn some features of this marvellous revelation.

Isn't this incredible? We are so weak, frail, unworthy. Yet God intends that we be one with Christ, the Lord of all creation. He desires us to have an intimate relationship with Christ, the kind of intimacy that is reflected in the relationship between husbands and wives.

This calls for sober thought. If we want to be true to God, we must set our heart on seeking to rise up to God's high calling of a deep and intimate relationship with Him.

RELATIONSHIP BETWEEN CHRIST AND THE CHURCH

The Church being Christ's body tells us of the spiritual union between Christ and the Church. In this most perfect of relationships, Jesus Christ is the "head of the Church", while the Church submits humbly to Him. He loves the Church and sacrifices His own life for her (Eph5:25). He sanctifies and cleanses the Church through His Word (Eph5:26). Jesus Christ presents her to Himself "in splendour", unmarred by any imperfection (Eph5:27). We are told that Christ loves the Church, and has made it pure and faultless by His death (Eph5:25-27). The apostle John's vision of the new heaven and the new earth describes the Church as Christ's Bride prepared and ready to meet her husband (Rev21:2).

The Church as "the body" of Christ was one of St Paul's favourite metaphors. He utilized it extensively in Romans, 1Corinthians, Ephesians, and Colossians. In the first chapter of his Letter to the Ephesians, St Paul says very much the same thing. "And He (God the Father) put all things in subjection under His feet, and gave Him (the Lord Jesus Christ) as head over all things to the Church, which is His body, the fullness of Him who fills all in all," Eph1:22-23. We have here the intimate relation of Christ with His Church described in these two aspects:

THE CHURCH IS A BODY OF WHICH CHRIST IS THE HEAD

We are the body of Christ. This "body" of Christ has both a "head" and "members" (Eph5:30). The "head of the body, the Church", is Christ Jesus. He is simultaneously the source, sustenance, and goal of all that exists (Col 1:15-18).

The Church is joined to Christ: We are "members of Christ" (1Co6:15); and, correspondingly, we are members of His body (1Co12:18, 20). To be a Christian is to be united with Christ Himself. The bodies of Christians are not their own, for "he who is joined to the Lord is one spirit with Him" (1Co6:17). Christ maintains the closest possible relations with His people. His ascension, instead of removing Him from us, by taking Him to a distant heaven, brings Him nearer to us, by His passing into the spiritual universe, through which He can have immediate contact with individual souls. In Eph5:28, St Paul says: "So husbands ought also to love their own wives as their own bodies." Christ loves, nourishes and cherishes the Church (Eph5:25, 29) because we are members of His body.

Likewise, Christians grow in Christ through service

in His body. The diverse gifts of the Church have their one source in the one God who is Father, Son, and Holy Spirit (1Co12:4-6). The diverse gifts are practiced through diverse members, and each is necessary for the proper functioning of the body (1Co12:14-22). Moreover, each member is granted unique honour (1Co12:23-25). Furthermore, each member shares in the life of the other members, both suffering and glorying together (1Co12:26). Just as our lives depend upon our participation in Christ, so Christians also are called to participate in His sufferings "for the sake of His body, which is the Church" (Col 1:24). Finally, God gave gifts to the members of the body, not for selfish reasons, but for her mutual "edification" or the "common good" (1Co12:7; 14:5).

There is one life in Christ and the Church: Christians also live with Christ through the ordinances He gave to His body. First, when Christians believe, it is a spiritual work inwardly, which should be subsequently seen in water baptism outwardly. "For by one Spirit, we were all baptized into one body," 1Co12:13; we were "buried with Him in baptism" (Col 2:12; Rom6:4).

Second, when Christians partake of the Lord's Supper, they immemorially participate in the very "body of Christ", in Christ and one another, "for we all partake of that one bread" (1Co10:17). Christians must learn to "discern the body" (their own, Christ's, and His Church) if they wish to avoid judgment in celebrating communion (1Co11:29). The same blood pulsates through the head and through the members of the body. The blood of Christ must not only be "applied to" Christians, as some people say, but "in them", drunk as Blood of Life (Jn6:56). Thus, by close communion with Christ in faith, submission, and obedience, the very life of Christ will flow through us, so that we can say, "Not I, but Christ lives in me." As the Church speaks truth in love, it grows in every way "into Him who is the head — Christ" (Eph4:15). Growing in life with Christ is why being a member of the body — the Church — is so important for Christians.

Christ presides over the Church: He is the Head of the body. The Church is not a republic; it is a kingdom, and Christ is its King. His thought teaches, His will commands, His Spirit gives Grace and order to all the movements of the body. The Church is subject to Christ in everything. Although there is this intimate love relationship between Christ and the Church, for it to work out well, the Church must be subject to Christ (Eph5:24). We cannot live as we wish, according to our inclinations and desires. We have to submit to Him as our head, our Lord. This is a key issue in Church life and in the fulfilment of God's purposes.

Because of the Church's failure to submit to Christ's lordship, many problems and much complexities arise. The Church becomes weak and impoverished. The more the Church fails to submit to Christ's lordship, the weaker it will be, and the easier it will be for it to be overcome by the evil one. There will be healthy growth of every believer and healthy growth of the whole body of Christ. The Church will then be able to fulfil its part well in the outworking of God's purposes as the Lord Jesus will lead and enable us in that direction.

The Church is one in Christ: The head has but one body. Though each one of us has an individual relationship with Christ, yet together, we are one unit in the spiritual realm. God sees us as one. As members of Christ's body, we complement one another in this spiritual organic reality. We will help one another so that we can fulfil the function that God has assigned to each one of us. It is like the human body, a metaphor that St Paul uses in 1 Corinthians 12. It is ridiculous for the mouth to be envious of the eye, and for the nose to be jealous of the tongue. Different parts of the body are necessary. They have different functions, and together they contribute to the proper functioning of the total person.

This applies not just to the local congregation, but also to the body of Christ worldwide. Because of the failure to see this reality sufficiently, many problems exist among God's people in different parts of the world and throughout Church history. If we truly appreciate our spiritual oneness, we will not have a spirit of envy, jealousy, strife and competition. Rather, we will complement and support one another.

Through Christ a common sympathy should spring up among Christians, just as, through their connection with the head, the various organs of the body co-operate harmoniously. When the influence of the head is lost, convulsions or confused movements are the consequence. So, sectarian enmity is a proof of severance from Christ. Nevertheless, variety is possible and even necessary in a highly organized body. There are many members, and all the members have not the same office. The essential unity consists in the subordination of all the parts to the one head.

Christ is the head of the Church: Our bodies are the limbs of Christ (Eph5:23; 1Co6:15; 1Co11:13). We are members of His Body (Eph5:30). Moreover, through her head, the Church is "nourished and knit together by joints and ligaments and grows with the increase that is from God" (Col 2:19). As the Church speaks truth in love, it grows in every way "into Him who is the head — Christ" (Eph4:15). Growing in life with Christ is why being a member of the body — the Church — is so important for Christians. This is indeed a profound mystery, a beautiful unity.

Jesus explained this wonderful unity in the example of the vine and the branches "Abide in Me and I will abide in you.... I am the vine; you are the branches," Jn15:4-5. The vine and the branches are one entity, like the head and the body. We abide in God as the branch abides in the vine, with the sap of the vine flowing into it and giving it life. If the sap of the vine does not flow into it, it dries up and dies.

The picture of the Church as a body, with Christ as its head, emphasizes that the Church is a living organism and not an organization. One of the characteristics of a living organism is reproduction or production of fruit. We cannot produce the fruit of the Spirit unless we abide in Christ. If we were to ask a branch on a grape vine, "How do you grow such luscious fruit?" the branch would probably reply "I don't know. I don't grow any of it; I just bear it. Cut me off from this vine and I will wither away and become useless." Without the vine the branch can do nothing. Jesus said, "Apart from Me you can do nothing," Jn15:5. As long as I strain and work to produce the fruit of the spirit from within myself, I will end up fruitless, and frustrated. But as I abide in Christ through obedient living, the Holy Spirit works in me to produce the fruit of the Spirit.

Separation from Christ is death to the Church. A Christless Church is a headless trunk. We may retain the doctrine and ethic of the New Testament, but, nevertheless, amputation of the Head means death. Even a partial severance of connection involves paralysis - loss of spiritual power and loss of spiritual feeling.

Christ is the Saviour of the Church: In Eph5:23, St Paul tells us that Christ is "the Saviour of the body". God has provided us full salvation in the Lord Jesus Christ. Salvation begins with conversion but goes beyond conversion. As we live our Christian life well, we enter more and more into full salvation in the Lord Jesus Christ. In the midst of spiritual attacks and many other difficulties of life, we look to Christ as our Saviour and Deliverer, and in the process, we enter more and more into what God intends for us in the Lord Jesus Christ.

So our primary concern should be to have a lively relationship with Christ and to seek to understand what is in His heart, and then to submit to His will and guidance.

Eph5:25 also tells us that Christ "gave Himself up" for the Church. The Cross exemplifies the depth and extent of Christ's love for us. We often think of Christ dying for individuals. While that is correct and biblical, it is not all there is. Eph5:25 emphasises not the individual, but the corporate aspect. Christ loved the Church and gave Himself up for her. In the plan of God, the Church has an essential part in the fulfilment of God's purposes.

We mean much to Him. We are valuable to Him. He loves us at all times. His love for us is not passive. It is one that continually seeks our good, our well-being. Therefore, we who love Him and walk with Him can have the deep assurance of His steadfast love for us. Christ loved the

Church and gave Himself up for her, so that He might sanctify her, and that He might present to Himself the Church in all her glory, holy and blameless.

God's goal for the Church is sanctification: "So that He might sanctify her, having cleansed her by the washing of water with the word, that He might present to Himself the Church in all her glory, having no spot or wrinkle or any such thing; but that she would be holy and blameless," Eph5:26-27. These two verses tell us that Christ is concerned for the moral and spiritual quality of the Church. He desires that the Church be sanctified, that she be holy and blameless, without any spot or wrinkle. He wants to present to Himself the Church in all her glory.

No doubt, Christ has already forgiven us and cleansed us. But we must move towards attaining God's high calling of moral and spiritual beauty. This is God's goal for the Church, and it is extremely important in the fulfilment of God's purposes.

THE CHURCH IS THE FULLNESS OF CHRIST

The "head of the body, the Church" is Christ Jesus. He is simultaneously the source, sustenance, and goal of all that exists (Col 1:15-18). The fullness of the deity dwells in Him, and He reconciles us with God through His death upon the Cross (Col 1:19-22). The complete life of God comes to the Church through her head (Col 2:9-10). All things in creation have been placed "under His feet", for God "gave Him to be head over all things". Through Christ's headship, we share fully in the divine life and in His rule. All things are "under" Christ and "to" the Church, "which is His body, the fullness of the One who fills all things in every way" (Eph1:22-23).

Christ's life thoroughly permeates the Church. It is filled with Christ. He is not only the Head above it; He is the life within it. He does not only teach, bless, command, and lead from without; He inspires His people and lives in His Church. Christ fills "all in all"; i.e. the Spirit that was in Jesus of Nazareth is in the whole universe, inspiring all creation and all providence with wisdom and goodness, purity and Grace. The same Spirit is in the Church. As yet, unhappily, the Church is not filled with Christ. Though Christ is received into the heart of Christians, every door within is not yet flung open to the gracious Guest. But in the perfect time, when His authority is everywhere established, His presence will be universally immanent.

In the ideal Church, Christ fills the affections with holy love, the thoughts with higher truths, the imagination with heavenly visions, the will with obedient actions. He fills all and His graces are seen in all. Already He begins the blessed indwelling. We look forward to His great triumph, when He will as fully fill His people as He will absolutely conquer His foes.

We are "the fullness of Him" (Eph1:23). In God's plan, in the fulfilment of His eternal purpose, we are to be an essential part of Christ. And as God works out His purposes through Christ, we, being the body of Christ, will also work out God's purposes together with Christ.

In summary, we see that the mystery of God is revealed in Christ through His Spirit, and He invites us to experience life with Him. He is an intimate God. The Father calls us to come "to" Him "through" His Son and "in" His Spirit (Eph2:18). He is our intimate God. He calls us to live from, in, and with Him, which also entails that we worship and serve with those who believe in Him. In this community, the Church, "we who are many are one body in Christ, and individually members of one another," Rom12:5.

Indeed, this mystery is great. What a wonderful revelation! What a privilege God has granted us! It requires spiritual insight to truly appreciate these realities.

St Paul wrote about praying for the eyes of the heart to be enlightened in order to properly appreciate what he is saying (Eph1:18). Let us pray that the Lord will grant us spiritual insight into the deep spiritual truths He has revealed.

"Fear not, little flock, for it is your Father's good pleasure to give you the kingdom. Sell your possessions, and give alms; provide yourselves with purses that do not grow old, with a treasure in the heavens that does not fail, where no thief approaches and no moth destroys. For where your treasure is, there will your heart be also," Lk12:32-34.

"Let your loins be girded and your lamps burning, and be like men who are waiting for their master to come home from the marriage feast, so that they may open to him at once when he comes and knocks. Blessed are those servants whom the master finds awake when he comes; truly, I say to you, he will gird himself and have them sit at table, and he will come and serve them," Lk13:22-30.

THE MARRIAGE SUPPER OF THE LAMB

According to the Jewish customs in Jesus' day, the Jewish marriage begins with the betrothal (St Joseph and St Mary, Mt1:18-19) which is a contract presented by the bridegroom to the intended bride and her father. After the betrothal, the young man would then give gifts to his beloved, and then take his leave. The young woman would have to wait for him to return and collect her. Before leaving the young man would announce, "I am going to prepare a place for you, and "I will return for you when it is ready".

The usual practice was for the young man to return to

his father's house and build a honeymoon room there. He was not allowed to skimp on the work and had to get his father's approval before he could consider it ready for his bride. If asked the date of his wedding he would have to reply, "Only my father knows." Typically, it would be a year before he came for his bride. Meanwhile the bride would be making herself ready so that she would be pure and beautiful for her bridegroom. During this time, she would wear a veil when she went out to show she was spoken for (she has been bought with a price).

When the wedding chamber was ready the bridegroom could collect his bride. He could do this at any time so the bride would make special arrangements. It was the custom for a bride to keep a lamp, her veil and her other things beside her bed. Her bridesmaids were also waiting and had to have oil ready for their lamps.

When they heard the bridegroom was coming, these virgins would go to meet him and light the way with their lamps. The lamp was either one with a small oil tank and wick or a stick with a rag soaked in oil on the end of it which would require occasional re-soaking to maintain the flame.

At the proper time appointed by the bridegroom's father a messenger would be sent to announce the bridegroom's coming and the bridegroom taking His wife. The bride not knowing when the bridegroom would come was to keep herself ready at all times.

When the groom and his friends got close to the bride's house they would give a shout and blow a shofar to forewarn the bride to be prepared for the coming of the groom. The guests would be invited to the wedding. Shortly after arrival, the bride and groom would be escorted by the other members of the wedding party to the bridal chamber. The bride would be adorned in her "wedding garments".

After nightfall, there would be a sacred procession through the streets to bridegroom's home. Everyone in the procession was expected to carry his or her own lamp. Those without a lamp would be assumed to be party crashers or even brigands.

The marriage between the bride and the groom would take place under a wedding canopy. The groom is greeted like a king under the canopy.

When the wedding party arrived at father's house the newlyweds went into the wedding chamber for a seven-day honeymoon and the groom's best friend stood outside waiting for the groom to tell him that the marriage had been consummated. Then all the friends really started celebrating for the seven days that the couple were honeymooning.

When the couple emerged there would be much congratulation and the Marriage Supper could begin.

Christ in the present age is preparing a place for His Bride. When this is complete and the Bride is ready, He will come to take the Bride to Her heavenly home which will be accomplished by the Rapture and translation of the Church at the end of the age. The actual Marriage Supper of the Lamb itself is specifically announced in connection with the Second Coming (the *epiphaneia*) of the Lord Jesus (Rev19:6-9).

"Then I heard what seemed to be the voice of a great multitude, like the sound of many waters and like the sound of mighty thunderpeals, crying, 'Hallelujah! For the Lord our

God the Almighty reigns. Let us rejoice and exult and give him the glory, for the marriage of the Lamb has come, and his Bride has made herself ready; it was granted her to be clothed with fine linen, bright and pure', for the fine linen is the righteous deeds of the saints. And the angel said to me, 'Write this: Blessed are those who are invited to the marriage supper of the Lamb.' And he said to me, 'These are true words of God'," Rev19:6-9.

As in Ephesians 5, here in Revelation 19, we see the Church in the glory and splendour of moral and spiritual beauty. We read in Rev19:8: "clothe herself in fine linen, bright and clean". This does not refer to physical linen and clothes. This refers to "the righteous acts of the saints". Some Christians think that righteousness is something that God just gives to us. But the phrase "righteous acts of the saints" suggests otherwise. It suggests that these are righteous acts carried out by righteous people. Yes, we cannot perform righteous acts by our own ability. We need the Lord's enabling. We need to cooperate with Him. Nevertheless, we can term these as our righteous acts.

Many believers are very busily trying to serve God, but

may not know what is in God's heart and how they can cooperate with God in attaining His purposes. We must cooperate wholeheartedly with the Lord to attain this goal – beginning with our own life and then contributing to the lives of others and the whole Church. Moral, spiritual beauty and stature of every believer and the whole body is the goal as well as the basis for effective service and contribution to God's Kingdom.

The great mystery was, that the eternal Son of God should form such a union with people; that He should take them into a connection with Himself, implying an ardour of attachment, and a strength of affection superior to even that which exists in the marriage relation. This was a great and profound truth, to understand. No one would have understood it without a revelation; no one understands it now except they who are taught of God.

Moreover, drawing upon the divine plan at creation for the marriage between a husband and his wife, St Paul pointed to God's design for husband and wife to "become one flesh" (Eph5:31-32; Gn2:24) to explain the relationship between the Church and her Lord. It is so intimate that nothing remains between the two of them: they have become one!

Relationship Between Christ And The Church

MYSTERY IN THE GARDEN OF EDEN

St Paul calls Gn2:24, "Male and Female He created them in the Image of God" to "become one flesh", a "mystery" because God did not reveal clearly all His purposes for the marriage of male and female in Genesis. There were hints and pointers in the Old Testament that marriage was like the relation of God and His people. But only when Christ came did the mystery of marriage get spelled out in detail. It is meant to be a portrait of Christ's covenant with His people, His commitment to the Church. Here is a mystery indeed.

That scene in Eden is also a parable. As God brought a bride to the first Adam while he was asleep in the Garden of Eden, God the Father sought a Bride for His Son from among the children of men. He took the Second Eve from the wounded side of the Second Man, as He lay asleep in the garden-grave.

To begin with, sinners are delivered from "the body of this death" through "the body of Christ" (Rom7:4, 24-

25). Christ's bodily resurrection altered the dynamics of creation, and Christians possess surety for their resurrection through His resurrected body (1Co15:20-23). The first Adam was a living being, but this second Adam, Christ, is "a life-giving Spirit" (1Co15:45). The resurrection life of the God-man is the source of life for believers. Redeemed men compose that Bride. The Saviour loves them, as a true man who for the first time loves a pure and noble woman. He does not love them because they are fair, but to make them so. He has approved His love by becoming man, and giving Himself to death. By His blood, and Word, and Spirit, He is sanctifying and purifying them for Himself. Both the justification and sanctification of the Church are from Christ, from the water and the blood which issued out of His side, when on the Cross.

The bringing and presentation of Eve to Adam has its analogy in the mystery. It was God that brought her to him; and she was the same that was made out of him; and to the same Adam was she brought of whose rib she was made, and that was not against her will. So, it is God that draws souls to Christ, and espouses them to Him, they are those that He has chosen in Him, and Christ has redeemed by His blood. They are brought to Christ, who was wounded for their transgressions, and bruised for their sins; and they are made willing in the day of His power upon them, to come and give themselves to Him. Adam's consent and acknowledgment of Eve to be his wife, foreshadow Christ's hearty reception and acknowledgment of the saints, as being of Him, and His, when they are brought to Him under the influences of His Grace and Spirit.

The process is long and severe; but He nourishes and cherishes them, as a man does his wounded flesh. And before long, when the Bride is complete in numbers and in beauty, the mystery that now veils her shall be flung aside, and amid the joy of creation, He will present her to Himself, without spot or wrinkle or any such thing. She will bear His name, sharing His rank, and position, and wealth, and power, and glory, for ever and ever.

Then the Church shall cleave to Him for ever, and He shall cleave to her. And the two shall be one spirit. And His own prayer shall be realized, offered on the eve of His agony and passion, "The glory which You have given Me, I have given to them; that they may be one, even as We are one," Jn17:22.

THE UNIVERSAL CHURCH

Everyone who has been regenerated in Baptism belongs to the body of Christ, the universal Church. The universal Church is manifested in the world by individual local Churches, each of which is to be a microcosm of the body of Christ. The Church is to function under the leadership of the Holy Spirit, operating under His sovereign rule. Jesus Christ is the Founder and Lord of His Church and has guaranteed its perpetuity until He returns.

The true Church of Christ is in intimate union with Christ Himself. It is indissolubly joined unto Him, vitally connected with Him, and, in addition, it is altogether His possession, His servant. When it is in sound and healthy condition, it is in profound and active sympathy with Christ in all His purposes and works; and when it appears in all its beauty and grace, it is in full conformity to the mind of Christ.

GOD'S GREATEST DESIRE

What is God's greatest desire for you? God sees you as a precious treasure, and He longs to have a close relationship with you. More than anything He wants you to have an intimate love relationship and fellowship with Him. God wants you to spend time with Him and intimately communicate with Him, to enjoy fellowship with Him, to trust and follow Him, and to give your life meaning and purpose by giving you the privilege of joining Him in His work.

Do you desire a deeper and closer relationship and fellowship with God? Is your desire to know Him and to please Him growing? Do you know that hearing God's voice is by far the most important part of your prayer and fellowship time with God? God needs to touch our hearts so that Jesus is our First Love, and so that we will faithfully and passionately seek Him and follow Him, however and wherever He may lead us.

It is a joy to Jesus when a person takes time to walk more intimately with Him. The bearing of fruit is always shown in Scripture to be a visible result of an intimate relationship with Jesus Christ. O, the fullness, the pleasure, the sheer excitement of knowing God here on earth. St Paul proclaimed, "I consider everything a loss compared to the surpassing greatness of knowing Christ Jesus my Lord, for whose sake I have lost all things," Php3:8.

As His bride, we experience intimate communion with Him now, while anticipating the wedding feast to come when the Groom will reveal Himself in all His splendour. As His body, we operate and cooperate as one whole unit, under the direction of the Head, to grow and function according to His purposes and to accomplish His assignments until His return.

We, the Church, are Christ's Bride and Body, and the Holy Spirit's temple. We are His because God made Himself ours. These images picture that glorious mystery of God's love for His people and the opportunity He has given for us to live and function in intimate fellowship with Him and each other, now and forevermore.

APPRECIATION
OF THE MYSTERY

The apostle Paul prayed that this great truth of "The Mystery of Christ" would become a reality for the believers in the Church at Ephesus.

"For this reason I bow my knees to the Father of our Lord Jesus Christ, from whom the whole family in heaven and earth is named, that He would grant you, according to the riches of His glory, to be strengthened with might through His Spirit in the inner man, that Christ may dwell in your hearts through faith; that you, being rooted and grounded in love, may be able to comprehend with all the saints what is the width and length and depth and height — to know the love of Christ which passes knowledge; that you may be filled with all the fullness of God," Eph 3:14-19.

To be strengthened with might through His Spirit in the inner man: St Paul asked that they would be strengthened with might, and that the strength would be according to the riches of His glory (a most generous measure). He also prayed that the strength would come through the Holy Spirit and that it would be put into their inner man.

There is an inner man just as real as our physical body. We all understand the importance of strength in our physical body, but many are exceedingly weak in the inner man.

According to the riches of His glory: God acts up to the dignity of His infinite perfections; He gives according to the riches of His glory.

That Christ may dwell in your hearts through faith: St Paul asked that Jesus would live in these believers, even as Jesus promised in Jn14:23: "If anyone loves Me, he will keep My word; and My Father will love him, and We will come to him and make Our home with him." Two ancient Greek words convey the idea "to live in". One has the idea of living in a place as a stranger, and the other has the idea of settling down in a place to make it your permanent home. Dwell uses the ancient Greek word for a permanent home. Jesus wants to settle down in your heart, not just visit as a stranger.

The glory of the indwelling Jesus is something for us to know, and to know by faith. It is there for us, but must be taken hold of through faith. We need spiritual strength to let Christ dwell within us because there is something in us that resists the influence of the indwelling Jesus. That something can be conquered as the Spirit of God gives us the victory of faith.

Being rooted and grounded in love: Two expressions are used: "rooted", like a living tree which lays hold upon the soil, twists itself round the rocks, and cannot be upturned: "grounded", like a building which has been settled, as a whole, and will never show any cracks or flaws in the future through failures in the foundation.

St Paul asked that all this would take place as they were rooted and grounded in love. The meaning seems to be that they should be rooted and grounded in their love for one another, more than being rooted and grounded in their love for God and the knowledge of that love.

May be able to comprehend with all the saints: St Paul asked that they might be able to understand together in community every dimension of the love of Jesus. St Paul wanted them to know it by experience and not just in words.

What is the width and length and depth and height of the love of Jesus: This means that the love of Jesus has dimensions and that it can be measured!

The love of Jesus has width. You can see how wide a river is by noticing how much it covers over. God's river of love is so wide that it covers over my sin, and it covers over every circumstance of my life, so that all things work together for good. When I doubt His forgiveness or His providence, I am narrowing the mighty river of God's love. His love is as wide as the world: For God so loved the world (Jn3:16).

The love of Jesus has length. When considering the length of God's love, ask yourself, "When did the love of God start towards me? How long will it continue?" These truths measure the length of God's love. "Yes, I have loved you with an everlasting love," Jer31:3.

The love of Jesus has depth. Php2:7-8 tell us how deep the love of Jesus goes: "but made Himself of no reputation, taking the form of a bondservant, and coming in the likeness of men. And being found in appearance as a man, He humbled Himself and became obedient to the point of death, even the death of the Cross." You can't go lower than the death of the Cross, and that is how deep the love of Jesus is for us.

The love of Jesus has height. To see the height of

God's love, ask yourself, "How high does it lift me?" It lifts me to heavenly places where I am seated with Christ. "He has raised us up together, and made us sit together in the heavenly places in Christ Jesus," Eph2:6.

Can we really comprehend the width and length and depth and height of God's love? To come to any understanding of the dimensions of God's love, we must come to the Cross. The Cross pointed in four ways, essentially in every direction, because:

- God's love is wide enough to include every person.
- God's love is long enough to last through all eternity.
- God's love is deep enough to reach the worst sinner.
- God's love is high enough to take us to heaven.

To know the love of Christ: St Paul wrote of something we can know. This isn't speculation, guesswork, emotions, or feelings. This is something to know.

That you may be filled with all the fullness of God: St Paul asked God to fill these Christians unto all the fullness of God. The word unto is a better translation than the word with. St Paul wanted Christians to experience life in Jesus Christ, the fullness of God (Col 2:9), and to be filled to their capacity with Jesus, even as God is filled to His own capacity with His own character and attributes. To be filled with God is a great thing; to be filled with the fullness of God is still greater; but to be filled with all the fullness of God utterly bewilders the sense and confounds the understanding!!!

WHO CAN BRING SUCH THINGS TO PASS?

It can only happen because God is able to do far beyond what we ask or think. Only God can do this because He can do far beyond our ability to think or ask (Eph3:20-21).

"Now to Him who is able to do exceedingly abundantly above all that we ask or think, according to the power that works in us, to Him be glory in the church by Christ Jesus to all generations, forever and ever. Amen." Eph3:20-21.

>  *You can ask for every good thing you have ever experienced – God can do above that.*
>
> *You can think of or imagine things beyond your experience – God can do above that. You can imagine good things that are beyond your ability to name – God can do above that.*

According to the power that works in us: God is able to do this in our life now, not beginning with heaven. This power works in us now. The things St Paul prayed for in the previous verses (spiritual strength, the indwelling Jesus, experiential knowledge of God's love, and the fullness of God) belong to us as children of God. However, they must be received by believing prayer and can be furthered in the lives of others by our prayers for them. When Christ is in you, He offers all of those glorious benefits. What a great God and Saviour we worship!

To Him be glory in the Church by Christ Jesus: The only fitting response to this great God is to give Him glory, especially in the Church, the company of His redeemed, and that He receive that glory throughout all ages, world without end. Amen!

ST PAUL'S CLAIM TO DIRECT REVELATION

The beginning of St Paul's Christian life was a revelation at the remarkable vision and communication on his approaching Damascus (Acts 9). He recognized his knowledge of the facts of Christ's life as directly communicated (Gal 1:11-12). He had no personal acquaintance with Christ; he was not dependent on the narratives of apostles and disciples, save in part (Gal 1:15-17). Christ told him His story by vision and revelation.

"For I received from the Lord that which I also delivered to you: that the Lord Jesus on the same night in which He was betrayed took bread; and when He had given thanks, He broke it and said, 'Take, eat; this is My body which is broken for you; do this in remembrance of Me.' In the same manner He also took the cup after supper, saying, 'This cup is the new covenant in My blood. This do, as often as you drink it, in remembrance of Me.'

For as often as you eat this bread and drink this cup, you proclaim the Lord's death till He come," IColl:23-26.

For I have received of the Lord that which also I delivered unto you: The information was thus miraculously bestowed on him by a direct call and revelation from the Lord Jesus. If St Paul had a distinct revelation on the matter of the Lord's Supper, we must regard it as a divinely instituted ordinance or sacrament and proof that St Paul had received a direct Divine revelation.

There were other times during his life of direct revelation, as at Troas (Acts16:7-10); in the temple at Jerusalem (Acts22:17-21); as declared by St Paul when in prison (Acts26:16-18); during the storm and shipwreck (Acts27:21-25); and as narrated in 2 Corinthians 12.

"Now when they had gone through Phrygia and the region of Galatia, they were forbidden by the Holy Spirit to preach the word in Asia. After they had come to Mysia, they tried to go into Bithynia, but the Spirit did not permit them. So passing by Mysia, they came down to Troas. And a vision appeared to Paul in the night. A man of Macedonia stood and pleaded with him, saying, "Come over to Macedonia and help us." Now after he had seen the vision, immediately we sought to go to Macedonia, concluding that the Lord had called us to preach the Gospel to them," Acts16:7-10.

On his way to Jerusalem to deliver the donations of the Christians in Asia, St Paul's ship was wrecked in a great storm. He saw a vision to encourage him about his safety and all the people on the ship.

"But after long abstinence from food, then Paul stood in the midst of them and said, "Men, you should have listened to me, and not have sailed from Crete and incurred this disaster and loss. And now I urge you to take heart, for there will be no loss of life among you, but only of the ship. For there stood by me this night an angel of the God to whom I belong and whom I serve, saying, 'Do not be afraid, Paul; you must be brought before Caesar; and indeed God has granted you all those who sail with you.' Therefore, take heart, men, for I believe God that it will be just as it was told me," Acts27:21-25.

St Paul was also known as "the Galilean, bald, with eagle nose, walking through the air to the third heaven" because of what he wrote in 2Co12:1-5.

"It is doubtless not profitable for me to boast. I will come to visions and revelations of the Lord: I know a man in Christ who fourteen years ago — whether in the body I do not know, or whether out of the body I do not know, God knows — such a one was caught up to the third heaven. And I know such a man — whether in the body or out of the body I do not know, God knows — how he was caught up into Paradise and heard inexpressible words, which it is not lawful for a man to utter. Of such a one I will boast; yet of myself I will not boast, except in my infirmities," 2Co12:1-5.

Most of the ancients, (except Origen,) as Clement of Alexandria, Justin Martyr, Irenaeus, Tertullian, and, among the moderns, Bull, Whitby, Bengelius, were of opinion that the apostle had two different raptures, because, as Methodius very well argues, if one rapture only were spoken of, the repetition of "whether in the body or out of the body" etc., would have been needless, when speaking of his being caught up into paradise.

If 2 Corinthians was written, as is commonly supposed, about the year 58 AD, then this occurrence must have happened about the year 44 AD. This was several years after his conversion, and of course, this does not refer to the trance mentioned in Acts9:9, at the time when he was converted. It is supposed that this vision was made to him when he was praying in the temple after his return to Jerusalem, when he was directed to go from Jerusalem to the Gentiles (Acts22:17). Others think it occurred after he was beaten and left for dead in Lystra (Acts14:19-20).

In both cases, the vision was to encourage him in the difficult and dangerous work in which he was engaged. Accordingly, by taking him up into paradise, and showing him the glories of the invisible world, and making him a witness of the happiness which the righteous enjoy with Christ, even before their resurrection, his faith in the promises of the Gospel must have been so exceedingly strengthened, and his hope so raised, as to enable him to bear with alacrity that heavy load of complicated evils to which he was exposed in the course of his ministry. Not to mention that this confirmation of the apostle's faith is no

St Paul's Claim To Direct Revelation

small confirmation of ours also. Some suppose that it was here the apostle was made acquainted with the mystery of the future state of the Church, and received his orders to turn from the Jews, and go to the Gentiles.

"And lest I should be exalted above measure by the abundance of the revelations, a thorn in the flesh was given to me, a messenger of Satan to buffet me, lest I be exalted above measure. Concerning this thing I pleaded with the Lord three times that it might depart from me. And He said to me, 'My grace is sufficient for you, for My strength is made perfect in weakness'," 2Co12:7-9.

Whether St Paul received the "Mystery of Christ" directly from Christ or heavenly things were brought down to him, in a trance, or state of ecstasy, or any other supernatural manner, he set forth the doctrine of Christ and on that foundation, the Church is built, and on that we must build our faith and hope.

> We have an awesome responsibility to make known the Mystery. Let us continue in the truth we have been taught and live the abundance that God has provided for us as members of the One Body.

The apostle Paul is God's evangelist par excellence and defender of the faith. Praise the Lord Jesus Christ for having commissioned to the Gentiles, one as Spirit-filled as St Paul. May we imitate St Paul in his Gospel-zeal to the glory of Christ. Amen.

www.ingramcontent.com/pod-product-compliance
Lightning Source LLC
Chambersburg PA
CBHW020752160426
43192CB00006B/309